THE CATHEDRALS
OF ENGLAND

By

HARRY BATSFORD
Hon. A.R.I.B.A., and
CHARLES FRY

With a Foreword by
SIMON JENKINS

Illustrated from Drawings by
BRIAN COOK
and from Photographs

BATSFORD

First Published May 1934

Reissued 2011, 2020

by Batsford
43 Great Ormond Street
London WC1N 3HZ

An imprint of Pavilion Books Group

ISBN 9781849945462

A CIP catalogue record for this book is available from the British Library.

26 25 24 23 22 21 20
10 9 8 7 6 5 4 3 2 1

Printed and bound by 1010 Printing International Ltd, China

This book can be ordered direct from the publisher at

www.pavilionbooks.com

FOREWORD

By SIMON JENKINS

The loveliest sight in England is from the foot of the stairs to Wells Chapter House. It rises in lofty symmetry to a forest of shafts, arches and traceried windows, like a ladder to Heaven. Half way up the visual symmetry breaks, the steps divide and they swerve gracefully to the right, into the exquisite chapter house chamber. Stop, says the architect, at this point in the ascent, there are delights to be had still here on Earth. Come see them. I know of nothing so beautiful.

Ten years after Harry Batsford and Charles Fry completed their guide to England's cathedrals in the 1930s, these places were considered doomed. A war-battered Church of England had to concentrate on reviving its parochial life and financing its clergy. Cities such as Bristol, Norwich, Durham and York had parish churches and to spare, all in desperate need of attention. Lesser centres, such as Ripon, Southwell, Ely and Wells, had no longer any use for places of worship of such size.

Even before the depradations of a bombing war, on a scale that Batsford and Fry could not have contemplated, the outlook for the cathedrals was grim. They were dinosaurs. The sense of reverential awe that infuses this guide might appeal to specialists. But what conceivable future could there be for these dinosaurs? They would have to pass to the state.

After the war Anglicanism continued to decline. The only area of growth was an evangelical movement with little time for churches, let alone cathedrals. In a lifetime of church visiting, I tired of hearing that "God's house is not a museum" and that worshippers were not art curators. The church commissioners remained adamant. Their business is to buttress the clergy but not buttress the roof over its head. If the public wants to keep its cathedrals, then the public had better look to its own resources. Commissioners are not conservators.

The pessimists were wrong. What has proved most unexpected, indeed astonishing, is that the public has supported cathedrals both as places of a new sort of collective worship and as great art. Of all institutions of the modern Anglican church, those in the most robust good health are its cathedrals. As Chaucer reflected with surprise on how "longen folk to go on pilgrimages," so we wonder at the appeal of cathedrals at a time when so much Christian worship is in decline.

England's medieval cathedrals, and indeed its modern ones, have worked their way into the nation's cultural consciousness largely independent of their function as religious shrines. They have been appreciated, locally, nationally and internationally, for what they manifestly are, one of the great art works of any age in any part of the world. Tourists appreciate them. Fundraisers love them. Support has also flowed to monastic structures that did not survive the Reformation settlement as cathedrals, and therefore do not feature in this book, such as Westminster, Selby and Tewkesbury. That the small market town of Beverley in Yorkshire might support not one great church but two is remarkable, yet it does.

The reason is plain from this book. Works that the Middle Ages erected to the glory of their God are appreciated today as glories of the Middle Ages. From Durham's stupendous arcade to the serene Perpendicular of York Minster, from Lincoln's lierne vault to the exuberant humanity of Exeter's bosses, from the intricate foliage of Southwell's capitals to Ely's majestic lantern, cathedral architecture and carving attained a quality unmatched down the centuries. Even visitors with little understanding of these arts cannot fail to gasp at the sight of Winchester's nave or the muscular strainer arches at Wells.

Glancing through these pages revives old controversies. Black and white pictures focus the eye on architectural form, undistracted by colour. The Romanesque nave at Peterborough undoubtedly has an austere dignity in monochrome. It is also intriguing to see old St Paul's in its uncleaned state, its portico gaining in depth and contrast. But I am reassured in preferring my cathedrals relatively scrubbed. The matt-black appearance of a gothic exterior, doused in coal dust, may carry a romantic patina of age for some, but it looks sooty and Victorian.

One happy consequence of the cathedral revival is restoration. Batsford's churches look dark places, as if sliding back towards the ruination in which the 19th century found them. Today they seem happier crowded places. While many, indeed most, local parish churches have been starved of attention and embellishment, cathedrals have taken on many of the civic and cultural functions they had before the Reformation. They are home to charities, regiments and guilds. They are used by schools and colleges: Canterbury is a glorious venue for Kent University degree ceremonies. Cathedrals are among the finest concert halls in the country. Their music schools are full and their choirs perform and record nationwide.

These places have rediscovered their place in the community and reasserted their primacy as beacons of England's religious, civic and cultural life. They are museums of all the arts without compare. This book is their worthy celebration.

SIMON JENKINS, 2011

PREFACE

This book is intended first and foremost as a compact pictorial review of the Cathedrals, with a brief account of each, written as simply and concisely as possible to meet the needs of the increasing body of people who appreciate these great churches, and are now, with the development of touring, able to visit them much more frequently and. widely. It is, of course, a large and fascinating field of study, capable of treatment from many angles and in almost infinite detail, and has furnished the subject-matter of quite a library since John Britton completed his great twelve-volume survey just over a hundred years ago. In fact, it may even be questioned whether any conspicuous need exists for yet another book: to which the answer is that, while the present volume cannot claim to provide more than a brief introduction on broad lines, most of the better works, such as Professor Prior's *Cathedral Builders* and Francis Bond's handbook, are out of print and no longer generally available, while in any case nearly all are planned on the generous pre-War scale that precludes reissue at a cheap price.

This book can, however, claim to illustrate the Cathedrals, if not in great detail, with all the resources of modern photography, with its transformed technique of lighting and effect. Actually there is in this office illustration material for an infinitely more comprehensive survey, that it only needs a measure of public support to produce; and since no such work has been published in England since Britton's time, it seems a pity that so fine a photographic documentation cannot be made available in some form or another without a prospect of financial loss. In any publication of the present size and price, it is naturally impossible to do full justice to the wealth of craftsmanship that the Cathedrals contain, but if the pictures provided awaken any new interest, or prompt people to go out and look at the originals for themselves, something will certainly have been achieved.

For the sake of completeness, the recent "parish-church cathedrals" have been very briefly included, though theoretically outside the scope of the survey, and a short Glossary of terms has been appended, which, though necessarily incomplete, may be of assistance in elucidating certain unavoidable technicalities. The drawings in the text have inevitably, in many instances, been submitted to severe reduction, in order to fit the space available in the description. Plans are given in the case of every 'major' cathedral, and these are reproduced to a uniform scale of 100 feet to the inch throughout to make comparison easy.

The excursions in connection with the book have covered many hundreds of miles, and we owe much to the patience and courtesy of the cathedral vergers who have led us conscientiously over roofs and up towers, along the dark ridge-passages of vaults and the giddy footwalks of triforiums and clerestories. The letterpress has had the privilege of a critical perusal by Mr. F. H. Crossley, F.S.A., whose valuable and caustic notes have been incorporated throughout, most particularly in the sections on Chester, Durham and Exeter. The section on St. Paul's has gained much from the suggestions of Mr. Gerald Henderson, the Sub-Librarian and Archivist of the Cathedral, and Mr. Aymer Vallance, F.S.A. has given us the benefit of his kindly advice on a number of difficult points. Finally, Mr. Edward Knoblock must be thanked for the practical expression of his interest.

H. B.
C. F.

April 1934.

THE DOUBLE-BRANCHING STAIR AT WELLS

PUBLISHER'S NOTE

The contents of this book is a faithful facsimile of the original 1934
text except for the new foreword by Simon Jenkins. As such, it includes
the phraseology of the time, descriptions of England's cathedrals of the
time, and also attitudes of the 1930s. We hope that this has a charm
and interest all of its own, but wish to remind readers that some of
the information in the book is now considerably out of date and also
that some of writers' opinions are not shared by the Publishers, and
no offence is intended. In particular we would like to mention that the
authors discuss the pre-war Coventry cathedral that was destroyed in
November 1940 during the Second World War bombing, and any
reference to the last century is the nineteenth century.

Historian and artist Hubert Pragnell has kindly checked the text and
below highlights those dated and/or incorrect pieces of information in
the book.

Canterbury Cathedral, page 17 'The roads approach through medieval
gateways'. Strictly speaking, there is only one medieval gateway over
a road, the West Gate. However, the cathedral is approached on foot
through the Christ Church gate c.1517.

Chichester Cathedral, page 27 The plan shows the Library located in
what is now the Lady Chapel. The Library was removed from the
Lady Chapel during the Cathedral restoration in 1871.

Durham Cathedral, page 30 Chapter House was extended to incorporate the eastern apse as one unit, not separate as in the plan used.

Gloucester Cathedral, page 47 The wooden figure effigy of Robert of
Normandy is no longer in the Quire. It was there from 1905–88 but
then moved to the south ambulatory where it is now.

St Paul's Cathedral, page 60 '....present reredos...'. This was destroyed
by a bomb on November 1940. It was replaced by a baldacchino or
canopy of marble and gilded oak over the new High Altar, based on
drawings by Wren, and completed in 1958.

Norwich Cathedral, page 66 The Lady Chapel was rebuilt as a memorial to the fallen of the First World War and is not located on the plan
provided.

Salisbury Cathedral, page 86 '...the vault at 85 feet to the ridge line is the highest in England'. This is not so. Westminster Abbey vault is 101 ft above the pavement of the nave.

Coventry Cathedral, page 112 The cathedral was, of course, destroyed by bombing in November 1940. The new cathedral was designed by Sir Basil Spence and completed in 1962.

Liverpool Cathedral, page 114 '....well on the way to completion by the mid nineteen forties'. It was finished in 1978.

Guildford Cathedral, page 114 The foundation stone was laid in 1936 but work was held up by the Second World War, and it was completed in 1961.

ACKNOWLEDGMENT

The publishers must acknowledge their obligation to the band of photographers whose work is reproduced in these pages, namely, Messrs. W. A. Call (The Cambria Series), of Monmouth, for Figs. 91, 95, 110; the late Mr. Brian C. Clayton, of Ross-on-Wye, for Figs. 12, 32, 34, 41, 57, 62, 63, 67, 82, 83, 85, 97, 101, 107, 108, 124; Mr. F. H. Crossley, F.S.A., of Chester, for Figs. 14, 15, 19, 31, 60; Messrs. Dawkes and Partridge, of Wells, for Fig. 109; Mr. Herbert Felton, F.R.P.S., for Figs. 20, 21, 26, 28, 71, 87, 90; Messrs. F. Frith & Co., of Reigate, for Figs. 4, 13, 24, 25, 30, 36, 46, 47, 80, 86, 105, 121, 123, 125, 131; Mr. W. F. Mansell, for Figs. 66, 73; Mr. Donald McLeish, for Fig. 61; the Photochrom Co., Ltd., for Figs. 22, 27, 37, 45, 81; Mr. Sydney Pitcher, F.R.P.S., of Gloucester, for Figs. 2, 10, 11, 54, 58; The Prussian Art Institute (*Photo-Abteilung des Kunstgeschichtlichen Seminars*), of Marburg-Lahu, Germany, for Figs. 44, 55, 94, 116; Mr. J. Dixon Scott, for Figs. 64, 120, 128, 129; Mr. Charles H. Stokes, of Exeter, for Fig. 51; the Rev. F. Sumner, for Figs. 89, 96; Mr. Will F. Taylor, for Figs. 3, 5, 6, 7, 8, 9, 17, 18, 23, 29, 33, 38, 40, 43, 49, 50, 52, 56, 59, 65, 68, 75, 76, 77, 78, 79, 84, 88, 92, 93, 98, 99, 100, 102, 103, 104, 106, 112, 114, 115, 117, 118, 119, 122, 126, 127; and Mr. W. W. Winter, of Derby, for Fig. 130. Figs. 53 and 111 were kindly supplied by the Great Western Railway Co., and Fig. 132 by the London, Midland & Scottish Railway Co. Figs. 113, 133 and 134 are included by courtesy of *The Times, The Builder and The Architect and Building News* respectively, and the colour frontispiece is reproduced, by permission of the authorities, from an original in the Victoria and Albert Museum, London.

CONTENTS

2 ANGEL PLAYING THE CITHOLE : Carved Stone Figure from the
Vault of the Gloucester Quire

3 WELLS : The 'Poor Man's Bible' of the West Front. A Plastic Framework for
one of the finest displays of Medieval Figure-Sculpture in England

INTRODUCTION

In the history of art in Western Europe, the building achievement of the Middle Ages provides in many ways the most remarkable chapter. In this country, in spite of the antiquarian researches of over a century, the extent of its surviving monuments is still seldom realised; and though it is customary to blame the Reformation and the religious struggles it engendered for a terrible programme of destruction, the fact remains that by far the greater proportion are church buildings since adapted to the sedate requirements of Anglican worship. Of these, the English village churches form a record of simple unpretentious craftsmanship flourishing in country places and reflecting the deep religious impulse and social outlook of a medieval peasant people. The greater parish churches of the towns represent a more complex and ceremonial way of living, the pride of gild and citizen and the keen local patriotism of a small world of rudimentary communications. The cathedrals are of loftier conception, crystallising the power and dignity of a rich and ambitious Church, yet revealing almost in every stroke of the mason's adze that latent other-worldliness inseparable from the workings of the medieval spirit.

The period of the Middle Ages can be reckoned arbitrarily as the thousand years that followed the collapse of the Roman Empire, roughly from 500 to 1500. A.D. For the first part of it, the spiritual currents of art and thought were feeble and intermittent, but from a phase of disruption and darkness a new building movement was evolved that took virile form in the so-called Romanesque style, which, fostered by the great Charlemagne at Aachen and the rising prestige of the Benedictine Order, began during the ninth century to spread itself gradually but impressively over Western Europe. Among the conflicting influences that worked on this youthful style, the old Roman tradition of the basilica, aisled and wagon-vaulted, was long maintained and developed, emerging as a logical and appropriate expression in round arcuated forms, which, despite a certain laboriousness in construction, was to hold the field for nearly four centuries with some magnificent achievements to its credit, a characteristic technique of ornament, and a powerful and vigorous school of sculpture. This style was introduced into England probably about a century and a half before the Norman Conquest, when many existing churches were rebuilt in stone. At first its practice must have been crude and provincial enough; at the same time it is a mistake to regard Saxon Architecture as other than a simple and more primitive version of the Anglo-Norman that superseded it, to which it had already been groping

1

its way slowly under potent pre-Conquest influences from across the Channel.

Though in many cases their religious foundations date from several centuries earlier, the history of the English cathedrals begins with the Conquest, when the unprecedented building wave that had already clothed Northern France with its "white robe of churches" finally swept over England. The majority of the cathedrals have at least a Norman core. Some, like Durham, Norwich and Peterborough, represent to all intents and purposes a Norman-Benedictine fabric, little altered at later periods, while others, as Exeter and Winchester, though rebuilt or transformed, still largely adhere to their Norman planning and proportions. By the middle of the twelfth century the style had reached its zenith in this country; but its maturity was short-lived. Already in the Île de France new tendencies were growing apparent that threatened to revolutionise previous architectural conceptions, and these, under the direction of a great creative innovator, the Abbé Suger, were crystallised in the new church then building at St. Denis, of which the consecration took place in 1144.

Northern France was the birthplace of Gothic Architecture and the Île de France its cradle. The innovations of St. Denis ran like wildfire through the small capital province, and there is nothing in history to compare with the mood of popular exaltation which, during the next eighty years, produced in superb sequence the cathedrals of Noyon, Sens, Senlis, Notre Dame de Paris, Laon, Bourges, Chartres, Rheims, Amiens and Beauvais. The new vernacular spread triumphantly through France, into Spain, Germany, England, and even as far afield as Cyprus and Sweden. For a generation nurtured on *pastiche* and revival, it is hard nowadays to realise the absolute unanimity of such a movement, and the spell that its productions cast over the popular imagination—a spell that remained potent until the first breath of humanism came to dissolve it like a mist that still clung reluctantly to the hollows. Gothic was first and foremost a folk art, expressing the physical and spiritual needs of a feudal and intensely religious people, and influenced by such powerful contemporary forces as Chivalry, the Gilds, and above all the majesty and ritual of the Church. Romantic and insistently linear in character, it was in its essence the art of the North, which, to some extent through the agency of the Crusades and of the cult of pilgrimages, had absorbed and utterly assimilated a group of complex Eastern influences; and it is a commonplace that it held the memory of the early forests. It was an art of craftsmen, not of aestheticians, an art that reached to uncanny heights of technical mastery through the heavy routine of bench and lodge, achieving at its summit a remarkable fusion of structural and spiritual aspirations. Constructionally it represented the spirit of collective adventure and exploration; its failures were crushing, its successes triumphant. It would never have admitted the psychology of small men bickering over Vitruvian precept; its master-craftsmen were grand extemporisers, but content by the canons of the times to work in anonymity, while the Church, the King or the patron took credit for the achievement.

And as an achievement it was staggering enough. It often seems as though the builders had actually competed in structural experimentation, aiming one beyond the other at an ever more emphatic verticality, an ever more daring economy of material; an ever vaster area for their lovely expanses of window, webbed with stone traceries and heavy with solemn colour. The introduction of the pointed arch brought into being the ribbed stone vault, its members gathered like sheaves into slender shafts rising through the three main storeys, its thrust counteracted on the outside by a scaffolding of flying buttresses, themselves steadied by a wealth of pinnacles. These, with the array of gables, tabernacles and buttresses with which the churches were literally clothed, produced an utterly new effect of fretted intricacy, beautiful from most aspects and perhaps most particularly in the bold semicircular sweep of the apse to eastward, rising superbly above its *chevet* of small chapels. But for the ordinary medieval man and woman, the chief wonder of the new cathedrals would be the sculptured caverns of their triple porches, with their range upon range of calm statues which seemed to breathe something of St. Bernard's quiet mysticism, a new spirit of gentle faith and solace far removed from the demonomania and threatening austerities of their Romanesque prototypes.

With the intimate connections between England and the Continent under the Angevin kings, it was inevitable that the germ of the new movement should develop rapidly in this country. Yet the evolution of Gothic in England was by no means identical with that of the Île de France, nor for that matter, in the early stages, was it comparable with it. At first only tentative local experiment followed the whole-hearted metamorphosis that was in progress across the Channel, and it was not until the opening years of the thirteenth century that English Gothic established itself as a consistent national architecture, from thence developing independently on its own lines until in its last long phase it emerged under its true colours as an utterly vernacular style, without Continental parallel or precedent. The chronological nomenclature of this architecture remains a vexed subject; and while no entirely satisfactory system has been produced, that of Rickman, with its six divisions based on the styles of window tracery, still seems, despite its obvious limitations, the most practical for ordinary purposes. Actually, of course, it was a continuous and living growth, with intermittent phases of activity and maturity, and its classification by 'periods' is bound to produce a slightly artificial impression. Nevertheless, these descriptive labels have their value if used circumspectly and within limits, and a classification by centuries is often far less satisfactory, if only in view of the gamut of change that most of them witnessed.[1]

The provenance of the cathedrals as they stand to-day is also rather complex and confusing. Nine of the pre-Conquest sees (Chichester, Exeter, Hereford, Lichfield, Lincoln, London, Sarum, Wells and York) were served at their seats by secular canons; and to these were added after the Conquest the great abbey churches of Canterbury, Durham, Ely, Norwich, Rochester, Winchester and Worcester, each with its quire of Benedictine monks, but containing, by an arrangement little known outside England, the throne of a bishop. Carlisle Cathedral was served by a foundation of Augustinian canons, and at the Reformation, the Augustinian churches of Bristol and Oxford were also promoted to cathedral rank, with the Benedictine abbeys of Peterborough, Gloucester and Chester. The great churches of the Cistercians, however, fared less fortunately at this period, for, by the rigid constitution of their Order, all were built, like Fountains, Rievaulx and Byland, in remote places, and were thus unsuited for conversion even into parish churches. The ruin of their austere Transitional architecture is one of the major tragedies of English building. The remainder are of comparatively recent establishment, and form a heterogeneous collection of abbey, collegiate and parish churches, though in two notable instances, Southwell and Ripon, the buildings had already long been used as supplementary 'bishopstools' necessitated by the vast area of the York diocese.

Similarly the fabrics, as will be seen in subsequent pages, form in the majority of cases a remarkable patchwork of building periods, sometimes piecemeal, and sometimes so incredibly composite that their dissection is a major and delicate operation. In certain of them, as Winchester, with its Perpendicular nave and Norman transepts, the contrasts are violent and abrupt; in others, such as Wells and Lincoln, there is a regular and harmonious gradation of styles, generally achieving its rich culmination in the eastern limb. Except in instances of clumsy patching and improvisation, which are not wanting, the effect, though often staggering to the foreign purist, is infinitely satisfying and delightful. In their diversity of form and detail, their calm aristocratic untidiness, the interiors elude description, and must be visited to be appreciated. Despite the vicissitudes of Church history, their wealth of craftsmanship is still almost inexhaustible; and together they form a vast and splendid memorial to some seven centuries of English labour in wood and stone.

*   *   *

The typical Benedictine abbey church built in England after the Norman Conquest was arranged on a consistent cruciform plan, evolved in line with the requirements of monastic worship. The long westerly limb was an aisled nave for the secular congregation,

[1] The subject of nomenclature has been fully and ably discussed by Professor Lethaby in his "Architecture" in *The Home University Library*.

4 DURHAM : The Piers of the Nave—perhaps the finest example of the
Anglo-Norman Building Style of the Eleventh and Twelfth Centuries

5   WELLS : The Nave Design of 1174. A magnificent early essay in
Gothic Building by a West-Country School

closed off from the monks' quire by a stone *pulpitum* or screen. Beyond it, the transepts were often built with eastern aisles for small altars, and over the crossing was usually a low tower surmounted by a short conical spire. The eastern limb contained the stalls of the monks and the sanctuary of the high altar, and the church ended eastward in either a trio of apses or a semi-circular processional ambulatory, with a series of radial chapels opening from it. Beneath the quire was a vaulted undercroft, or crypt, where the saints' relics in the possession of the monastery were exhibited. The cloister was almost invariably on the sheltered south side, between nave and transept, with the monastic buildings grouped around it in an arrangement generally similar in its essentials to that of Durham, shown in the plan on page 30.

Something of the strength and dignity of these interiors emerges in the photographs of the Durham, Norwich and Peterborough naves on Figs. 4, 35, 76 and 80. But their present severity belies the smooth perfection of their original finish with a thin coating of plaster over all, clothing them on the outside in immaculate white, and on the inside forming the basis for an elaborate scheme of mural painting in bright diapers and figure pieces cognate in style with contemporary manuscript illuminations. The little St. Gabriel's Chapel in the crypt at Canterbury, the fragments of wall paintings that survive at St. Albans (89), Chichester and Winchester, and the great diapered ceiling of the Peterborough nave, recall something of the pristine beauty of this decoration. Nevertheless these churches, though built on an unprecedented scale, were on the whole reticent in carved ornament, of which their range was limited to a few motives, though the luxurious decadence of the Cluniac Order brought a new decorative richness into the work of the earlier twelfth century, little represented among the cathedrals, however, save in the working of individual capitals and of heavily sculptured door tympana, as at Rochester and Ely (*page 36*).

At the same time, as the century advanced, signs were apparent all over the country of an impending break with Romanesque formula, which, though long ignored with typical conservatism by the Benedictines, found expression in some interesting Transitional experiments of local schools, as at Ripon (*page 77*), Worcester (this as early as 1140) (*page 104*), and above all in the virile independent style employed by the conversi, or lay builders, of the Cistercian Order for their northern abbey churches of Fountains, Kirkstall and Furness. The precise currents on which Gothic Architecture was borne into England provide an obscure and controversial problem much beyond the scope of this book; but it is certain that its development must not be attributed to any single stream of influence, nor must it be forgotten that while a French master-mason was supervising the erection of the Canterbury quire, an English school of the West Country was working out its own interpretation of the same ideas in the nave at Wells (5). St. Hugh's quire at Lincoln (*circa* 1190) provides at once the culmination of the Transitional phase of the twelfth century and the inauguration of the building programme of the thirteenth in this country; and it is significant that the favourite English use of Purbeck marble from the Corfe quarries for shafting and string-courses, clumsily employed at Canterbury, here achieves its first maturity.

With the thirteenth century, the English builders established their national idiom, which, if not to be compared in grandeur or daring with the style current in France, had its own distinctive grace of adolescence, finely represented, despite later falsification, in the cathedrals of Salisbury, Lincoln and Wells. Here are churches conceived on a new scale of splendour, but independent of monastic influence and purely as the seats of bishops, expressing, over and above their ritual message, something of the princely dignity of the prelate-statesmen concerned in their building, as Poore at Salisbury, Grosseteste at Lincoln and Jocelyn at Wells. Their planning marked a definite departure from the old tradition, and involved a transformation of the eastern limb, with a general enlargement of the presbytery to provide fuller accommodation for the canons; while beyond the high altar, a processional path gave access to an eastern extension, or retro-quire, built to house the feretory and treasure of the local shrine, now brought above ground from the crypt. Small eastern transepts were often constructed to provide additional altars for the canons' daily masses, and with the rising English cult of Our Lady, a Lady Chapel of lower elevation was generally added to the extreme east. A result of these alterations was entirely to abolish the original scheme of apses, and to substitute the square terminations so characteristic of English Gothic (100). Certain features, however, were generally retained from the monastic arrangement, such as the cloister, now chiefly used for Sunday processions, and the chapter-house, usually built, following a precedent established at Lincoln, as a spacious well-lit polygon, loftily vaulted from a central pier.

Professor Prior has well characterised this English style as it emerged with the thirteenth century as "an art of slender shaftings of Purbeck marble, pointed lancets, wall arcades ranged one behind the other, level-crowned vaults, with multiplied string-courses of marble, arch-molds of many members, some adorned with the dogtooth, and often with a free and varied carving of white stone in label-heads and capitals—and finally it had a splendid free figure-sculpture. So we have it at St. Hugh's Cathedral at Lincoln and at the Ely Galilee, then at Salisbury, and in all the great works of the thirteenth century in England." Though generally effective and consistent in the design of its façades, it seldom rose to striking monumental heights save in the great sculptured screens of its west fronts, embracing such dissimilar triumphs as Peterborough and Wells, the latter conceived as little more than a framework for the display of some of the finest figure-carving in England, a

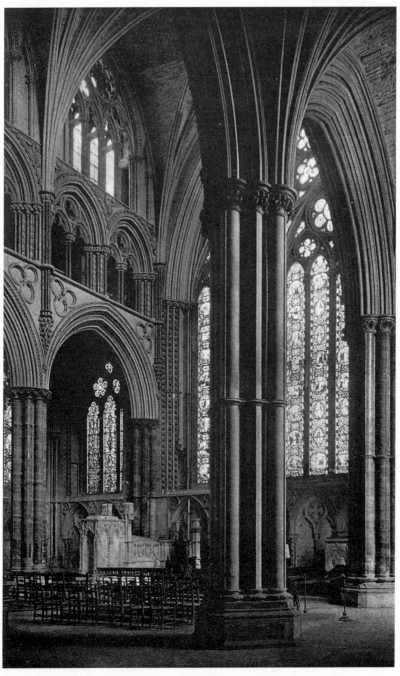

6 LINCOLN : The 'Angel Choir,' looking East. The Culmination of the Style
of the Thirteenth Century in England

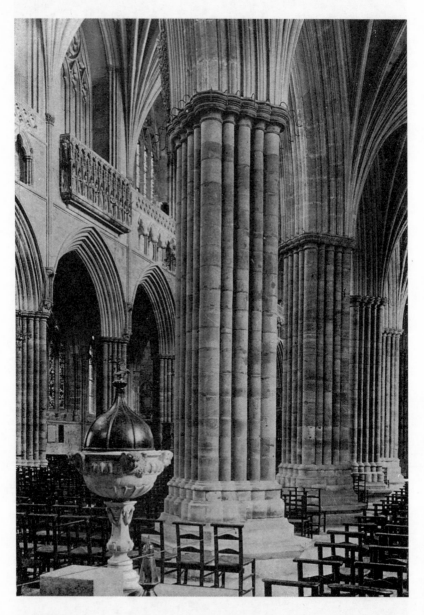

7 EXETER : The Nave, built in the rich exuberant style of the earlier Fourteenth
Century. Notice the Musicians' Gallery in the Triforium, with its carved Angel
Orchestra, and the Seventeenth-Century Font in the foreground

plastic revelation by west-country craftsmen of the didactic aims of medieval religious art. The effect on the peasant mind of this eloquent 'poor man's Bible,' with its sombre lower panels of the Doom, must have been overwhelming in the sunlit beauty of its original polychrome (3). The style may be reckoned to have reached its summit towards the close of the century, when the lancets and plate tracery of its fenestration were gradually superseded by larger windows patterned at their heads with the precise stone cuspings and circles that characterise the *Geometrical* phase. The cathedral of Lincoln is perhaps the best barometer of thirteenth-century change, and its culmination eastward in the famous 'Angel Choir' (*circa* 1280) not only displays the full maturity of this art in England, but is prophetic of the rich development of the next century (6).

'Geometrical' does in fact mark the transition from the formal seriousness of thirteenth-century art to the romantic luxuriant style of the fourteenth century that succeeded it. As a development, this latter was inevitably influenced by the picturesque if rather super-ficial brilliance of the English Age of Chivalry, when the circle of Edward III and his sons was emulated in every Court in Europe; and its predominant constructional discovery was the ogee arch, enhanced by crocketing and applied as a favourite motive in the rich ornamental elaboration of the surface treatment. While Geometrical elements were sometimes retained in the window tracery, as at Exeter, there was a more general relaxation into free *flowing* or *curvilinear* forms, that constitutes one of the most intriguing and individual developments of English Gothic. Such gaily imagina-tive achievements as the east window at Carlisle (27) and the west window at York (122) are without Continental parallel; their rich colour seems quickened as with a flickering of wings. Accomplished local schools emerged in East Anglia, where the curvilinear fashion persisted well into the next century, and in the North, where the west front of York Minster was built with a riotous luxury unpre-cedented even at its period (122). Generally speaking, however, this manner is somewhat sparsely represented among the cathedrals, though the naturalistic revolution in carving found expression in the springtime exuberance of certain smaller works, such as the Southwell Chapter-house and the Lady Chapel at Ely. But the outstanding achievement was at Exeter, where a famous line of building bishops left a triumphant monument to the skill and fecundity of local craftsmanship in an interior which, in its sensuous warmth of molded marble and luxuriance of freestone carving (7), brings a worldly and almost pagan note into Gothic Architecture.

The catastrophe of the Black Death of 1349 spelt the virtual extinction of this rich school. But already, before the blow fell, the masons of the Severn Valley had been sowing the seeds of their revolution, that found its first expression in the recasing of the old Romanesque core of the Gloucester quire in *circa* 1340 with

C

a delicate rectilinear scaffolding of light masonry (8), and its unifica-
tion into a lofty single-storey design, crowned by a clerestory of tall
windows that formed in effect a continuous stonework lantern.
The events leading to this consummation are described in another
chapter (*page* 44); its results were far-reaching, for it inaugurated
a system of economical yet almost consistently effective surface
treatment that was to endure in England longer than all the previous
Gothic styles combined. In the period of exhaustion that followed
the pestilence, this new *Perpendicular* manner found immediate
adoption; well before the end of the century it was used with
notable effect for the large scale reconstructions of the Winchester
(9) and Canterbury (21) naves, while in 1549 it was flourishing, and
even as late as 1649 was still occasionally employed in such strongholds of conservatism as the Universities of Oxford and Cambridge.
Though the achievement of the Gloucester quire was never quite
surpassed, the maturity of the style is expressed delightfully in the
little Lady Chapel (55) of the same cathedral (*circa* 1470), which
typifies in miniature the English churches and chapels of the fifteenth
century, lofty rectangular halls, aisleless, and built to all intents and
purposes of panelled glass, roofed either with intricate lierne vaults
or the lovely national development of fan vaulting, another child
of the Gloucester cloisters, that reached its triumphant manhood
in the retro-quire at Peterborough (81) and the magnificent later
chapels of St. George at Windsor, King's College at Cambridge
and Henry VII at Westminster. But the province of Perpendicular
that left its most conspicuous mark on the cathedrals was its craft
of tower-building, that produced, as the last splendours of waning
Gothic, the grand exuberant piles that raise their heads over the
central spaces at York and Gloucester, Worcester and Canterbury,
with their burden of deep-toned bells that were already, by the
close of the fifteenth century, tolling the decline of medieval ways
of life, art and thought in this country.

*   *   *

It remains to write something of the manner of men responsible
for the building of these churches—a subject embracing the difficult
problem of the medieval architect, and the complexities of masonic
craft organisation, that can only be treated summarily in this
chapter. In the full spate of the *furor Normanorum* of the eleventh
and twelfth centuries, hordes of unskilled workmen were employed
by the monks on their abbey churches to supplement the limited
supply of professional masons, and to this fact is due the rough,
rather hasty character of much Romanesque masonry intended for
a plaster finish, and the subsequent disintegration and structural
failure that are part of the records of most English cathedrals.
At first this labour was housed in the monasteries and organised
under strict monastic discipline, but it is a fallacy to suppose that
in the ordinary course of events the religious themselves took any

8 GLOUCESTER : A Detail of the Quire Reconstruction that worked the
Perpendicular Revolution. The old Norman core is overlaid with a delicate rectlinear
scaffolding of light masonry. The shrine of Edward II can be seen screened off in
the central bay, and in the foreground is the early effigy of Robert of Normandy

9 WINCHESTER : Another Perpendicular Recasing of a Romanesque Core. A
view in the North Nave Aisle at the Crossing. The central pier is uncompleted, and
shows the original fabric of the Norman arcade, once covered by a screen

10, 11 WORCESTER : Late Medieval Tomb Carvings. The Bishop on the right
is from one of the encrusted vertical members of Prince Arthur's Chantry, shown in
Fig. 12. On the left is St Anne teaching the Virgin to read

13 WINCHESTER : William of Wykeham's
Chantry in the Nave

12 WORCESTER : Prince Arthur's Chantry in the
South Aisle, with a Glimpse of the Quire

active part in the work. By about the middle of the twelfth century, however, the craft seems to have achieved a measure of independence, and for the first time to have organised its own lodges adjoining the work in progress, directed by a class of skilled *magistri cementarium*, or master-masons, to whose credit the evolution of medieval structural design undoubtedly belongs. In the words of Professor Willis, "they were perfectly practical and ingenious men; they worked experimentally; if their buildings were strong enough, there they stood; if they were too strong, they also stood; but if they were too weak, they gave way, and they put props and built the next stronger. That was their science, and very good practical science it was too."

Despite their high technical accomplishment and the burden of responsibility they shouldered, it may be taken as a general rule that, not at any rate until after the Black Death, when a master-mason's services were at a premium and craftsmen had actually to be empressed for the royal works, did these men attain to any higher status in society than that of senior and trusted artisans; and a long spell of good service might be rewarded by a retiring post such as gatekeeper of the completed building. Few of their names have come down to us from the earlier centuries; nevertheless it was they, in the face of difficulties and obscurities that would have overwhelmed lesser men, who have the cathedrals largely to their credit, and the famous sacrists, priors and even bishops who in the past have been loosely credited with individual achievements, can seldom have been responsible for more than the business organisation of the work, together with the provision of building materials, which, of itself, in the appalling state of communications, often demanded a high talent and enterprise. At first the materials were worked almost entirely on the spot—the busy scene presented by any great building in course of erection is depicted in the illustration (16). But from the first, the popular Purbeck marble of thirteenth-century building was an exception, being dressed and molded at the Dorset quarries; and as the century advanced, the practice of specialised 'shopwork' in local centres became increasingly common, as with the alabaster tombs of Derbyshire and the Norfolk fonts. There is reason to suppose that the carved angel orchestra in the spandrels of the Lincoln quire was delivered piecemeal and assembled, rather carelessly in certain instances, on the spot; and by the end of the fourteenth century, it may be assumed that the majority of carving and decorative work beyond the ordinary was delivered in sections from the great craft workshops already established in the leading cities.

The workmen were latterly of two grades, the freemasons, who undertook the more highly specialised and ambitious work of freestone carving, and the rough hewers, who dressed the stone blocks, cut moldings, and were generally responsible for the plainer fabric of any Gothic building. To the freemasons, together with the carpenters, who, during the later centuries, rose to almost equal prominence, we owe the magnificent range of craftsmanship of which the cathedrals, despite the vicissitudes of Reformation, Civil War and opiniated restoration, are still the repositories. The fertile art of the stone-carver is apparent in the working of capitals, corbels, arcading, label-terminations, the figured bosses of ribbed vaulting, pinnacled tabernacle-work and niches, and the like, and in the splendid English funeral craft of tombs, monuments and chantries. The schemes of colour decoration have vanished, and of the glories of stained glass that largely survived the Reformation, much was smashed by Puritan zeal at the time of the Civil War, though what remains in fine windows at York, Canterbury and elsewhere testifies to the excellence of the native craft. Towards the close of the fourteenth century, carpentry reached its zenith in this country, communicating something of its rich delicacy to the stone-carver's technique. The stallwork of Lincoln, Chester (15) and Manchester, with its deft notation of misericords, marks the florescence of this craft among the cathedrals; but the tradition of skilled excellence endured beyond the Reformation, and we see it recurrent in Bishop Cosin's lovely Carolean font cover in the Durham nave (36), and later in the carving of Grinting Gibbons and his fellows at St. Paul's Cathedral. Finally, despite the jeremiads of nineteenth-century Gothicists, it is cause for infinite rejoicing that the cathedrals preserve their fine range of Renaissance monuments, that carry the story of craftsmanship almost down to our own times—or at least to the *débâcle* of 'church-furnishing' during the later Gothic Revival.

If, as may be argued, the English cathedral builders seldom achieved a logical *tour de force* comparable with an Amiens or a Beauvais, they did at least contribute through the centuries to the evolution of a distinctive national creation, of which many of the salient features are without parallel outside this country. As compensation for the soaring height that made the French vaults marvels of audacious construction, there is the infinite complexity of later English roofing, with its utterly national development of the fan vault, and the intricacies of the polygonal chapter-house. The level vistas along the roof-lines of the mighty English naves have a beauty of their own, as, on the outside, have the long low lines of the cathedral ranges, broken at the west and centre by the rich magnificence of their later towers, grouping superbly against their green landscape background. Their weather-tinged faces have the calm of weariness, and something of their repose has communicated itself to their surroundings of unruffled lawns and quiet prebendal houses hidden among old trees. Worn and ageless as they stand, these great buildings are not the least part of our national heritage; their careful preservation in their last state is incumbent on a public now awakening to their intelligent appreciation.

15 CHESTER: The Quire looking West, showing the Return Stalls of 1380, with their rich Entrance Canopy

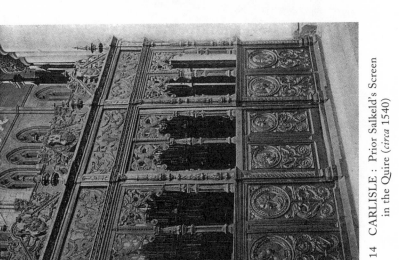

14 CARLISLE: Prior Salkeld's Screen in the Quire (*circa* 1540)

16　FIFTEENTH-CENTURY BUILDERS AT WORK. Notice in the
Foreground the Mortar-Mixer, the Bricklayers, and the Masons cutting Moldings
on Stone Blocks

BRISTOL

Though of the medieval buildings only the quire and transepts survive, and these have suffered considerable alteration at later periods, much of the design is so original and unusual that the work is of the highest interest. Only some scraps in the fabric remain of the original Norman church of the founder, Robert Fitzhardinge; but the chapter-house, completed to a rich design following a grant by Henry III in 1155 of the forfeited estates of Robert de Berkeley, survives, though the great Norman gateway to College Green was rebuilt to its original design in 1515. During the thirteenth century, the original, now the 'Elder' Lady Chapel, was added east of the north transept; but the great period of reconstruction was under Abbot Knowle (1306-1337), which saw the evolution of the present quire, with its aisles and presbytery, and the little sacristy on the south side. Under his successor, Snow (1332–1345), was added the Berkeley Chapel adjoining the latter, and the Newton Chapel off the south transept. The central tower was raised by Abbot Newland, or Nailheart, in *circa* 1500.

Owing to the destruction of the documents in the chapter-house by a riotous 'Reform' mob in 1831, a chronicle of Nailheart's time preserved at Berkeley Castle is now the chief source of information concerning the abbey's history. The extraordinary severity with which the Black Death raged at Bristol, and the consequent decimation of the monks, probably precluded the resumption of the work begun on the nave under Abbots Snow and Newland, and Abbot Elliot (1515–1526) is credited with its demolition. His death, and the subsequent Dissolution, put an end to schemes of rebuilding, and the church remained without a nave until 1868, when the work was completed to the late G. E. Street's design. The beautiful sixteenth-century screen was arbitrarily removed by Dean Elliott in 1860, but portions have now been re-erected as a parclose. Pearson's restoration of 1892 was responsible for the repair of the Elder Lady Chapel, the rebuilding of the central tower and the replacement of various quire fittings.

It is unnecessary to attempt a detailed analysis of the exterior, as the main features of the design can be most advantageously grasped from within. Street's nave and towers do not blend badly with the fourteenth-century eastern limb, though the west front is a rather mechanical composition that smells of the lamp. Crowned by its burly central tower, the cathedral is seen to its best advantage from the lower ground to the south (17), and externally the absence of a triforium and clerestory is very marked, though the tall double-tiered windows of the quire form a fine range. Of the interior, the little Elder Lady Chapel is a pleasant early work, with a Geometrical east window and characteristic wall-arcading, carved in the spandrels. But it is in the design of the quire that the bold originality of the fourteenth-century school of Bristol masons becomes immediately apparent. This is unique among the cathedrals in that the aisles are of equal height to the main building (19), though a somewhat similar arrangement occurs at the Temple Church in London, and further afield in Anjou. Non-clerestoried churches, of course, swarm in the South-West, but these are not vaulted. Here at Bristol, while the main vault is of simple type (18), those of the aisles are complex and absolutely unique. From each pier, a solid stone beam or transom is thrown across the aisle (19), sustained by a pointed arch beneath, with pierced ovals in the spandrels. From the centre of each transom springs a slender inverted pyramid of ma-sonry rising to ridge ribs on either hand which form a series of small in-dependent lateral com-partments. This arrangement, possibly more remarkable for its ingenuity than for its beauty, was followed by Street in the aisle vaults of the nave. It forms an interesting early experiment in a novel technique of skeleton ma-sonry construction that was to reach its culmination in the remodelling of the Gloucester quire, possibly by the same school of craftsmen, a few years later.

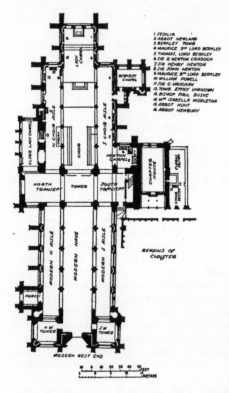

I SEDILIA
2 ABBOT NEWLAND
3 BERKLEY TOMB
4 MAURICE. 3ᴿᴰ LORD BERKLEY
5 THOMAS, LORD BERKLEY
6 SIR R NEWTON CRADOCA
7 SIR HENRY NEWTON
8 SIR JOHN NEWTON
9 MAURICE, 9ᵀᴴ LORD BERKLEY
10 WILLIAM POWELL
11 SIR C. VAUGHAN
12 TOMB. EFFIGY UNKNOWN
13 BISHOP PAUL BUSHE
14 Mᴿˢ ISABELLA MIDDLETON
15 ABBOT HUNT
16 ABBOT NEWBURY

LADY CHAPEL
BERKLEY CHAPEL
ELDER LADY CHAPEL
N CHOIR AISLE
S CHOIR AISLE
CHOIR
NEWTON CHAPELS
NORTH TRANSEPT
TOWER
SOUTH TRANSEPT
CHAPTER HOUSE
CLOIR VESTRY
CLOISTER
MODERN N AISLE
MODERN NAVE
MODERN S AISLE
REMAINS OF CLOISTER
PORCH
N W TOWER
S W TOWER
MODERN WEST END

The delicate openwork vault of the sacristy was another original contribution of this school, which was quickly imitated at St. Davids, as was the ornate stellar canopy work which is a feature of the Bristol tombs. Of these, that of Abbot Newland is the most splendid, with its five large radiating and richly crocketed 'spokes.' The position of the altar-screen (a modern substitute by Pearson) has been a good deal shifted, but it has now been returned to its original place, with space for a processional path and an unaisled Lady

17 BRISTOL : The Cathedral from the South-East

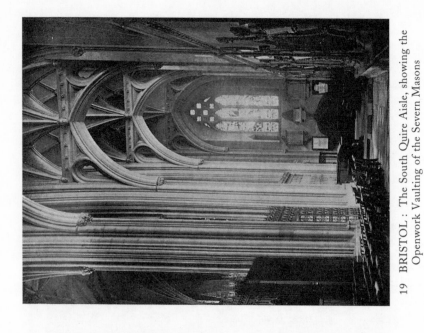

19 BRISTOL : The South Quire Aisle, showing the Openwork Vaulting of the Severn Masons

18 BRISTOL : The Quire looking East. Pearson's Reredos largely obscures the Curvilinear East Window

Chapel of two bays to east of it, which preserves its own original fourteenth-century reredos. The great east window is of striking curvilinear design (18), with some original glass in its upper lights, and incorporated in the modern stalls is a series of vigorous medieval misericords. The Norman chapter-house, of which an eastern bay was probably demolished, is richly arcaded and vaulted, but other remains of the monastic buildings are few and fragmentary.

THE TOMB OF ABBOT NEWLAND IN THE LADY CHAPEL

CANTERBURY

The first basilican church given by King Ethelbert to St. Augustine, with its relics of St. Wilfrid, St. Dunstan and St. Swithun, was destroyed at the time of the Conquest. Work on a new cathedral and Benedictine abbey was begun in 1070 under Lanfranc, the first Norman archbishop—an unambitious scheme of building hurriedly completed in seven years and based on that of the Conqueror's own abbey at Caen, from which Lanfranc came to rule at Canterbury. It was not long before this church became quite inadequate for the seat of the primate and a quire of over a hundred monks, and by direction of Archbishop Anselm the eastern limb was enlarged and entirely remodelled between 1096 and 1115 under Priors Ernulph and Conrad, much of whose work is still visible on the outside. But the glory of 'Conrad's Quire' was short-lived. In 1174 it was gutted by fire; and it was possibly significant for the course of English Gothic that among the crowd of *artifices* assembled by the monks, a Frenchman was chosen as master-mason for the reconstruction, William of Sens, who may or may not have been concerned in the building of his native cathedral a few years earlier. The degree of French influence in the design of the new quire as it emerged has been the cause of much controversy; Professor Prior saw in it "not quite the character of the Cathedral at Sens, and only a half-hearted attempt at the Gothic which the French masons had achieved," while Mr. Bond described it roundly as "made in France." The fact remains that, four years after the commencement of the work, the master was disabled by a fall from the scaffolding, and his place taken by one William the Englishman, who completed it six years later in 1184. Though the most cursory examination of the rising style of the Île de France discloses the French elements in the Canterbury design—the great projection of the buttresses, the characteristic lancets, coupled columns, arch-molds and Corinthianesque capitals, to say nothing of the setting-out of the whole—there is at the same time much that is indigenous and prophetic of the English vernacular of the next century, notably the enthusiastic employment for the first time of brown Purbeck marble for detached shafting and string-courses, and a rising school of Caen freestone carving. When it is remembered that the monks had directly stipulated that their quire was to be rebuilt on the old Anglo-Norman lines, the task of analysis becomes still more complex. The final assumption must be that the work as it stands represents a compromise, not uncharacteristic of English cathedral art, between the wishes of the patrons, the natural proclivities of a French master-mason, and the irrepressible instincts of native craftsmen consciously or subconsciously working out the matter for themselves.

Four years before the fire that had necessitated this rebuilding had occurred the most significant event in the medieval history of the cathedral, namely the murder of Becket in 1170. The story is too familiar to need repetition, but the fame of the martyr spread rapidly through Europe, and his shrine at Canterbury became one of the most popular places of pilgrimage of the Middle Ages. In 1220 the relics were translated from the crypt to the Trinity Chapel east of the high altar with almost Byzantine ceremonial, and for the next three centuries a stream of pilgrims, including kings, princes and cardinals, with crowds of the poor and diseased and those prosperous 'middling' people so neatly drawn by Chaucer, flocked to the shrine, with offerings ranging from the carbuncle jewel the size of an egg laid there by Louis VII of France to the halfpence in the palm of a beggar. Even in the early sixteenth century, when the offerings had considerably diminished, the annual income was over £4000 (an immense sum for the period), and the great Erasmus, visiting the shrine, remarked how "the meanest part was gold, every part glistened, shone and sparkled with very large jewels, some of them exceeding the size of a goose's egg." Late in the fourteenth century the monks decided at last to rebuild Lanfranc's archaic nave and transepts, and the present work was carried out under Prior Chillenden between 1379 and 1400. The Lady Chapel and so-called Warrior Chapel were added during the next century, and between 1495 and 1503 the lovely central tower was raised to replace the original Norman 'Angel Steeple.' With the Reformation, Henry VIII issued his famous writ against Thomas Becket for "treason, contumacy and rebellion," which was read before the shrine in 1538. The suit was tried at Westminster, and in the absence of a defendant had its inevitable sequel in the removal of the gold and jewels of Canterbury in twenty-six cartloads to the royal treasury. Henceforward Henry wore the *régale* of France on his own thumb. Such treasures as had escaped the Reformation were for the most part destroyed by Puritans in 1642 under the notorious 'Blue Dick,' though by something like a miracle a portion of the magnificent early glass remained undamaged. Since the Restoration the fabric has been carefully tended and preserved, and has on the whole suffered little at the hands of modern restorers.

The cathedral lies in a saucer of green hills; and some of the loveliest views of it are to be had from the crests of the roads leading into the city, as at Harbledown, where Chaucer's party made its last halt, and pilgrims were accustomed to fall on their knees at first sight of the golden angel above the tower. "Tanta majestate sese erigit in coelum," wrote Erasmus, recording an impression with an unaccustomed note of emotion, "ut procul etiam intuentibus religionem incutiat." To-day the angel has vanished, and the city

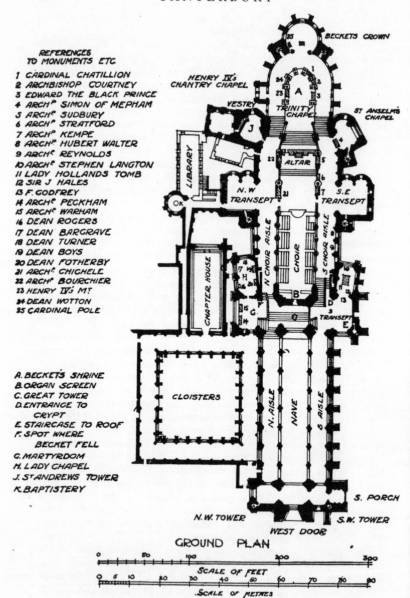

REFERENCES
TO MONUMENTS ETC

1 CARDINAL CHATILLION
2 ARCHBISHOP COURTNEY
3 EDWARD THE BLACK PRINCE
4 ARCHᴾ SIMON OF MEPHAM
5 ARCHᵉ SUDBURY
6 ARCHᴾ STRATFORD
7 ARCHᴾ KEMPE
8 ARCHᴾ HUBERT WALTER
9 ARCHᵉ REYNOLDS
10 ARCHᵉ STEPHEN LANGTON
11 LADY HOLLANDS TOMB
12 SIR J HALES
13 F. GODFREY
14 ARCHᵉ PECKHAM
15 ARCHᵉ WARHAM
16 DEAN ROGERS
17 DEAN BARGRAVE
18 DEAN TURNER
19 DEAN BOYS
20 DEAN FOTHERBY
21 ARCHᴾ CHICHELE
22 ARCHᴾ BOURCHIER
23 HENRY IVᵗˢ Mᵗ
24 DEAN WOTTON
25 CARDINAL POLE

A. BECKET'S SHRINE
B. ORGAN SCREEN
C. GREAT TOWER
D. ENTRANCE TO
   CRYPT
E. STAIRCASE TO ROOF
F. SPOT WHERE
   BECKET FELL
G. MARTYRDOM
H. LADY CHAPEL
J. ST ANDREWS TOWER
K. BAPTISTERY

BECKETS CROWN
HENRY IVˢ CHANTRY CHAPEL
VESTRY
ST ANSELM'S CHAPEL
TRINITY CHAPEL
LIBRARY
J
OR
ALTAR
N.W. TRANSEPT
S.E. TRANSEPT
N CHOIR AISLE
S CHOIR AISLE
CHOIR
CHAPTER HOUSE
TRANSEPT
E
CLOISTERS
N. AISLE
NAVE
S AISLE
S. PORCH
N.W. TOWER
S.W. TOWER
WEST DOOR

GROUND PLAN

SCALE OF FEET
SCALE OF METRES

must have spread its bounds, though not a great deal, about the
cathedral, rising pale and shapely above the rooftops, its three tall
towers grouping magnificently against their background of Kentish

20 CANTERBURY : The Cathedral from the South-West

21 CANTERBURY : The Nave looking East, showing the Carolean Font

fields and woods. The roads approach through medieval gateways, and a network of narrow busy streets of overhanging houses, old inns and rather forlorn little parish churches surrounds the broad *enceinte* of what was one of the greatest and richest of European abbeys, of which considerable remains exist, partly in ruins or in the structure of later buildings. The Canterbury close is indeed one of the most fascinating architectural mazes in England, and it is a morning's task to explore with a plan its several green courts and walled alleys, its ruined arcades and pleasant Georgian canons' houses.

The fabric of the cathedral itself is of a complexity of style and texture that it would be difficult to analyse adequately in many pages. The west front of *circa* 1440 is an effective and well-proportioned composition as it stands, though later houses prevent a view to its best advantage, and the north tower is of course a rebuilding of 1834 to replace the Norman stump that appears in Britton's engravings, that was probably the last considerable portion of Lanfranc's church. Chillenden's nave forms a fine and lofty Perpendicular range (20), with probably the tallest aisle windows in England, and the same design is carried into the transepts, where the great windows are of a spacious and striking beauty, that in the south flanked by a single rich pinnacle. Rising to 235 feet above all (20), the slender central tower, 'Bell Harry,' is unsurpassed of its type, a splendidly exuberant achievement in the cheerful English craft of tower-building, which seems to refute at its close the pessimism of the exhausted fifteenth century. Beyond the transepts begins the earlier complex amalgam of the quire buildings, and here generally speaking the small intersecting arcades, the form of the shallow chapel-apses, and the delightful pair of arcaded towers against the eastern transepts belong to Conrad's work of 1115, while the graceful ranged lancets, crowded into couples as they curve around the apse, and the tall thin buttresses, show the French tinge. The contraction of the east end, as apparent from without as from within, was due to the small Norman chapels of St. Andrew and St. Anselm that still cling to the presbytery, the latter with a large and very beautiful fourteenth-century window inserted, reminiscent of Kentish type. The building terminates eastward in the remarkable culmination of the Corona, or Becket's Crown, which remains an architectural puzzle. Lacking its final storeys, it has never been discovered how it was intended to complete this rather gaunt curving tower of Gallic lancets and lofty emaciated buttresses, which stands unfinished and ending, so to speak, in the air.

Entering at the west, the Perpendicular nave of nine bays, though conspicuously short for England, is a work of consummate grace and refinement (21), built with a slender economy of stonework that lends spaciousness to its actually moderate dimensions. The natural comparison is with the Winchester nave, which is

practically its contemporary; but while at the latter the Norman
core necessitated close spacing and solid construction, the Canterbury builders had free scope to indulge a whim for lightness which
if anything is rather carried to excess in the finished work. The
elongation of the piers at the expense of the upper storeys can
certainly be criticised, and, as a result, the main lighting has to be
effected from the tall triple-stage aisle windows. In point of fact
it is a two-storeyed design, for the triforium represents no more
than the lower stages of the clerestory windows, plainly panelled
in stone, with glazing only in the traceried upper lights. The main
arcade, together with the light lofty vaults of nave and aisles,
springs from shafts grouped against the molded piers, each with its

SOUTH VIEW OF THE QUIRE, SHOWING ST.
ANSELM'S CHAPEL AND THE CORONA TO THE
EAST

small neat independent capital. Except in the west window, little
original glass remains, and there are few fittings beyond the gaily
painted Carolean font (21), though the aisle walls are covered with
a motley of tablets and monuments that recalls Westminster.

The crossing affords the most beautiful views of the cathedral (23).
Broad flights of steps ascend to the quire level, and the arches are
spanned by rich 'girders' of pierced and cusped stonework, dear
to the hearts of Perpendicular builders (21). Poised above all
hangs the delicate fan-vault of the tower, sparingly touched with
colour; and, to north and south, the lofty transepts end in immense Perpendicular windows of silvery and warm-hued glass, that
in the north incorporating the figures of Edward IV at prayer
with his wife and family, and the little princes done to death by

22 CANTERBURY : A View of the Quire from the *Pulpitum*, looking
eastward to Trinity Chapel

24 CANTERBURY: The Ambulatory of Trinity Chapel, showing the varied marbles of the coupled columns

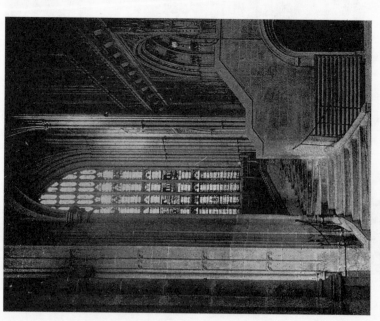

23 CANTERBURY: A View at the Crossing, looking to the North Transept, or Martyrdom, with the Royal Window of Edward IV

Richard III (23). Here in the north transept Becket fell, but little remains from his period save the actual flagstones, and its name, the Martyrdom, which has persisted through the Reformation. Opening out of it to the east is the beautiful little fan-vaulted Lady Chapel of *circa* 1450, with its rich fourteenth-century screen; and corresponding on the south side, the famous Warrior Chapel is crowded with picturesque monuments and roofed with a complex lierne vault of Gloucester type (25).

The dim ill-lit quire (22), under its heavy vault, needs little further discussion here. Beyond its high evolutionary interest, the signs of immaturity and compromise are easily apparent, and as a finished work of architecture it cannot bear comparison with St. Hugh's quire at Lincoln or the nave at Wells, which are so nearly its contemporaries. The stone *pulpitum*, with its interesting royal statues, is of the fifteenth century, and on the interior, the return stalls have a splendid range of Late Renaissance canopies of circa 1700. The remainder of the fittings are modern, but the quire is enclosed by a stone screen added by Prior de Estria in 1304–1305, and the aisles reveal traces of a gracious scheme of painted decoration. A broad flight of steps ascends to the high altar (22), now stripped of its reredos, which extended between the presbytery pillars at the narrowest point of contraction. East of it is the simple impressive horse-shoe of the Trinity Chapel, with its apsed ambulatory of French type around an arcade of coupled Corinthian pillars (24), built of a variety of stones and marbles that were probably the gifts of individual foreign donors. The site of Becket's shrine behind the high altar is now only marked by its pavement of Alexandrian mosaic, brought back from the East by the Crusaders. Here also in the south arcade is the fine simple monument of the Black Prince, with its metal effigy and bitter Norman-French inscription, beneath a wooden tester bearing traces of the original painting. His helmet, surcoat and scabbard (the sword has vanished) are hung above him, and his shield is fixed to the pillar close by. Facing him across the church lies his son's usurper, Henry IV, with his wife, Joan of Navarre, their small fan-vaulted chantry opening from the aisle beside the tomb. At the east end, the Corona forms a lofty circular chapel, lit by lancets, which contains the archaic stone chair in which the English primates are enthroned.

The crypts beneath form a remarkable series that to all intents and purposes reproduces the ground plan of the eastern limb. The major quire crypt is the work of Ernulph and Conrad, and incorporates some unusual Romanesque capitals and diapered piers. Beneath the south-east transept is the Huguenot chapel where the service has been said in French each Sunday since the reign of Elizabeth, and the crypt of St. Anselm's Chapel has its own little apsidal chapel of St. Gabriel, preserving fresco paintings that give some general idea of the old medieval splendour of this world beneath a world, with its glimmering altars and chantries, and

E

in the centre the fabulous treasure of Our Lady described by Erasmus, which was only revealed to privileged eyes. The eastern apse
beneath the Trinity, with its round pillars and central vaulting

shafts, is a beautiful little
church in itself (26), and belongs to the later building.

A second chapter could
be written on the profusion
of monuments, medieval and
later, with which the cathedral is crowded; the Lady
Chapel and Warrior Chapel
(25) in the transepts are in
themselves an epitome of the
English funeral craft at its
best. Nor is it possible to do
justice to the windows that

ROMANESQUE CAPITAL IN THE CRYPT   make Canterbury the greatest
treasury of early stained glass in
England. These are for the most part of the deep-toned medallion
glass of the thirteenth century, probably from the *ateliers* of Chartres
itself, and the best specimens occur in the north quire aisle, the
Trinity Chapel, and in the eastern lancet of the Corona. Many fragments are also incorporated in good modern facsimile work, and
there are some beautiful expanses of the silvery glass of the fifteenth
century, notably in the great window of the south transept. The
conventual remains are too extensive for adequate description, but
mention must be made of the ruined arcade of the infirmary, with
its chapel and miniature cloister, the interesting circular 'lavatory
tower,' or conduit, and the Norman staircase in the close. The rich
fourteenth-century cloister is very dilapidated, but the chapter-house
is preserved in good condition, a spacious rectangular chamber reconstituted under Chillenden, with large windows and an interesting
painted wooden ceiling.

FROM THE HILLS TO THE NORTH-WEST

25 CANTERBURY : The Warrior Chapel adjoining the South-West Transept, with the tombs of Lady Holland and her two Husbands; Sir Thomas and Lady Thornhurst (recumbent); and Colonel Prude (kneeling)

26 CANTERBURY : The Eastern Crypt beneath the Trinity Chapel

27 CARLISLE : The Quire and the great East Window

CARLISLE

The cathedral stands on high ground near the castle, islanded, with the green patches of its close, in a rather grim and shabby industrialism. Though only its head and shoulders survive, there is much to command admiration, and one supreme achievement in its east window (27). The first church was begun by a Norman priest, Walter, whom Rufus had appointed governor of the city in 1092, and was completed by Henry I, who endowed a priory of Augustinian canons to serve it. Ten years later it became the seat of a bishop. The Norman quire was reconstructed on a larger scale during the thirteenth century, and, with extension only possible to the north, is out of line with the nave. A series of minor fires was responsible for a good deal of early alteration, culminating in 1292 in a destructive blaze that spared only the vaulted aisles of the quire, and brought about the fourteenth-century transformation. Six bays of the nave have vanished, traditionally demolished by the Parliamentary garrison in 1645 to repair the city fortifications; and, in 1745, Jacobite prisoners herded in the cathedral did inevitable damage to the interior. It is a matter for satisfaction, however, that despite the vicissitudes of the war-scarred Border town and an extensive restoration by Christian in the eighteen-fifties, the cathedral still retains much of its admirable range of old fittings.

The west front is necessarily a patch, and of the stern Norman design of the old nave, only a fragment of two bays remains, with the west wall of the south transept. The façades of the transepts, together with the north and south doors (the latter now the principal entrance to the cathedral), are modern reconstructions; and the central tower, rebuilt by Bishop Strickland in 1392, is unassuming, but owing to irregularities in its planning, tricked out with two stair-turrets to fill the space. The contrast between the Romanesque severity of the nave and the lightness of the quire is enhanced by the use of a pleasant red sandstone for the latter as against the cold grey texture of the earlier fabric. The few Perpendicular aisle windows have been arbitrarily replaced by modern lancets, but the ranges of the clerestory afford some compensation in their imaginative diversity of flowing tracery forms. The east front is a graceful and dignified composition almost filled by the immense curvilinear window of nine lights that is the building's glory (27), with a lesser triangular window in the gable above.

On the interior, the Norman nave design is carried on into the south transept, opening from which is the little chapel of St. Catherine, with Prior Gondebour's screen of the later fifteenth century, one of the most exquisite in England in its lace-like delicacy of detail. The quire aisles are of thirteenth-century design, with plain quadripartite vaults, a cusped wall-arcade and profuse dogtoothing. The main arcade retains its thirteenth-century arches, beneath which, after the fire of 1292, the fourteenth-century builders, by skilful underpinning, inserted new piers, with a fine display of naturalistic carving in the capitals, now largely remodelled, including a series of fieldwork through the Seasons. The triforium is delicately treated in trios of small two-light cusped openings, and the curvilinear clerestory windows rise above a graceful parapet of pierced quatrefoils. The great east window is a masterpiece of its type (27), in the words of Rickman, "by far the most free and brilliant example of Decorated tracery in the kingdom," comparable only with the west window at York, which it excels. While the glass of the main lights is modern, that of the tracery is contemporary and very beautiful. The quire is roofed with a timber barrelvault from which stray ham-merbeams project—relics of some earlier unfulfilled intention. The stalls are sound fifteenth-century work, if lacking the imaginative brilliance of Chester or Manchester, with misericords that comprise quite a part of a medieval Bestiary; the thistles and other emblems cut on their woodwork are relics of Scottish prison-

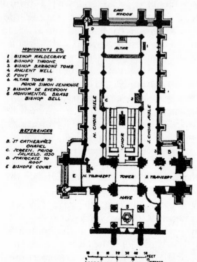

ers held in the cathedral in 1598. On the north side is the beautiful Renaissance screen of Lancelot Salkeld (14), last prior and first dean of the cathedral, which dates from *circa* 1542.

The monastic buildings were almost entirely reconstructed under Prior Gondebour during the fifteenth century, but the majority of these, together with the cloister, were demolished, probably at the same time as the nave. There remains, however, a large fratry with a vaulted undercroft—now used as chapter-house, library and choir school—containing an attractive little reader's pulpit, with a staircase ceiled with cusped circles. The prior's lodging has been enlarged to form the present Deanery.

CHESTER

The monastic church at Chester was founded in 1093 by Hugh
Lupus, Earl of Chester and Lord of the Welsh Marches, for the
Benedictines, and dedicated to St. Werburgh. It was made a
cathedral by Henry VIII—one of the few public gifts during his
bleak reorganisation of the Church of England—and is attractive
in retaining constructionally so much of what it stood for to its
former occupants. Its monastic buildings far exceed in interest the
remodelled, over-faced and bookishly renovated church from which
the scaffolding was again removed towards the close of the nineteenth century (28). The peculiar plan was the outcome of its
position in a small walled city, the north-east corner of which it
occupied with little room for expansion. When it became necessary
to enlarge it, the cloisters precluded development to the north, and
the city to the west. Thus the lengthening proceeded east and then
south, taking in the parish church of St. Oswald, which was adapted
as a south transept of five bays, double-aisled. The monks built the
congregation a new church without the precincts, the remains of
which now form the shell of a cinema, but the dispute entailed by
their action continued throughout the Middle Ages, and even
beyond the Reformation.

The cathedral is built of red sandstone, and down the ages the
fabric has suffered from the soft friable nature of this material,
entailing continual patching and recasing even in medieval times.
Of the founder's church, only the north transept has survived, with
the lower stages of the north-west tower and the north wall of
the nave aisle. The first great period of rebuilding was between
circa 1200 and 1315, when the eastern limb was remodelled with a
new Lady Chapel; but with the fourteenth century, the monks
again set about enlargements which included, besides the adaptation
of St. Oswald's, the reconstruction of the nave and central tower
(28). This work, however, was interrupted by the Black Death, and
not resumed until late in the next century, when its design was considerably modified under Abbots Simon Ripley (1485–1498) and
Birkenshaw (1498–1537). The interior is generally warm and
mellow in tone, with some fine effects of lighting; but there is a
certain gauntness about the nave, a two-storeyed design with a
well-proportioned arcade slightly richer on the north side, and
a footwalk running beneath the clerestory windows instead of a
triforium (29). The Norman north transept has seen many changes.
When the shrine of St. Werburgh (of which the base now rests in
the Lady Chapel) became the chief financial asset of the abbey, it

was evidently placed in it to enable the populace to give their alms
without encroaching on the quire reserved for the Community.
The Norman arch to the east chapel, recently reopened, was built
up, and the transept fenced by a heavy stone screen, of which a
fragment remains in the east corner. The quire, largely of *circa* 1300,
is, like so much at Chester, a somewhat composite work, also virtually
of two storeys, with a triforium of blind cusped arcading and a

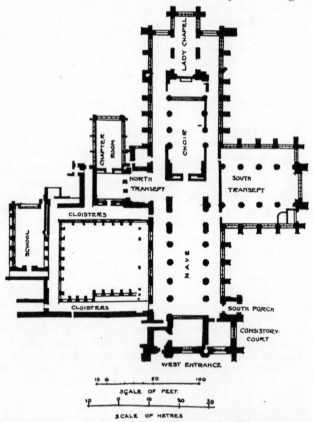

passage around the lofty clerestory windows behind a parapet of
cusped quatrefoils. Its woodwork is the cathedral's chief glory.
This has been moved several times, but its proper position is under
the tower, where the piers have been corbelled away to contain it,
and a wide plain wall left for the *pulpitum*. The canopied and pinnacled stallwork remains largely as executed with the exception
of the front pillars, which have been cut away, spoiling the upward
growth of the design. It was erected in 1380, ten years after the
work at Lincoln, on which it forms a distinct advance, and retains

28   CHESTER : The Cathedral from the South-East, showing the Quire,
Central Tower and part of the South Transept, formerly the Church of St Oswald.
The candlesnuffer roof in the foreground was introduced by Scott

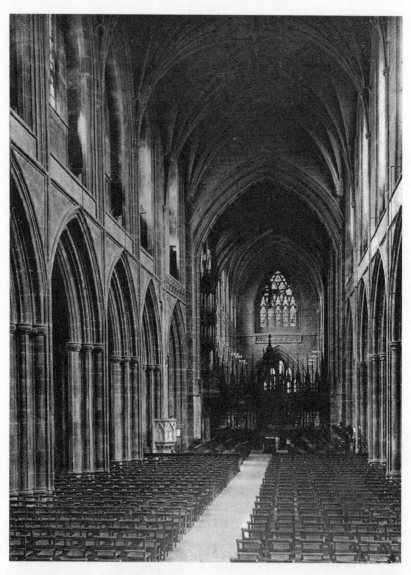

29 CHESTER : The Nave looking East, with the profile of the Return Stalls

a superb series of misericords, illustrating fables, scriptural scenes and incidents from the medieval Bestiaries. The entrance to the quire preserves its mass of pinnacled detail (15), but the *pulpitum* has been removed, though a portion of it now backs the stalls in the north aisle.

The recently renovated cloister, its vault and stonework conservatively repaired and the windows glazed, emanates a feeling of continuity and use, and is the centre of diocesan activity. The garth is now a flower garden, from the centre of which the monastery tank has been excavated, originally supplied with water by lead pipes from Christleton, two miles away. Leaving the cathedral by the north-east processional doorway, the first door on the right leads to the chapter-house vestibule, its thirteenth-century vault supported on slight columns entirely without capitals—a peculiar and graceful novelty of the time. The chapter-house itself, also of the thirteenth century, is rectangular in plan, with tall lancet windows, having a footwalk at the sill level. Here many of the treasures of the cathedral are stored, and the cupboard incorporates the fine scroll ironwork of Thomas de Leighton, who was also responsible for the grille before the tomb of Queen Eleanor in Westminster Abbey.

Continuing, we pass the slype leading to the infirmary and cemetery, and through the next trefoil-headed doorway on the right are the day-stairs to the dormitory, now destroyed, lit by two quatrefoil windows. Immediately beyond is the parlour, its early vault supported by three piers, now used as a library and for small meetings. Turning left, we pass the remains of the monks' lavatory in the north alley, with the entrance to the refectory immediately beyond. This fine room, long used as a classroom by the Grammar School, has encountered many vicissitudes. Cut short by a dean to make a convenient passage from his house to the cathedral, it has now been restored to its full length, and is used for meetings and hospitality. It retains its beautiful pulpit, from which readings were given during meals, the only others of its kind in anything like a complete state being at Beaulieu and Shrewsbury, the latter a fragment now cared for in a garden.

The slype adjoining led to the kitchens. Turning left, we enter the west alley, bordered by the Norman undercroft, originally partitioned as cellars and the monks' warming-house. Above it was the abbot's lodging, but all that remains of this is the chapel overhanging the cloister at the south-west corner, of Norman construction, with a sanctuary added by Bishop Bridgeman in the seventeenth century, who covered the barrel-vault with ornamental plasterwork and added a screen. In this cloister are the carrels, formerly wainscoted into small closets for study. Turning left again, we are in the south alley-way, entirely rebuilt by Scott, also with carrels, the south Norman wall recessed with arches to contain the volumes borrowed by the monks for their study.

CHICHESTER

For its setting Chichester Cathedral has one of the most charming old towns in England, placed in the flat Sussex country between the wooded ridge of the South Downs and the sea. Moderate in its dimensions, it stands in a narrow strip of green churchyard, with a cluster of old houses on the south side; and the exterior shows plainly the heterogeneous character of the fabric (30), most of the work in which can be assigned within a period of roughly two centuries, between *circa* 1091 and 1305. The former date marks the commencement of the first Norman church under Bishop Ralph de Luffa a few years after the transference of the old Saxon see of Selsea to Chichester, and its dedication took place some twenty years later, though it is doubtful how far the work had advanced at this period. It is certain, however, that the church was already completed with its nave at the time of the fire of 1187, which caused serious damage to the fabric and was responsible for its re-roofing with a plain stone vault throughout, necessitating a general adjustment of the design. Another result was the remodelling of the two eastern bays of the presbytery to an interesting Transitional design (34), in which Purbeck marble played an important part, under Bishop Seffrid II, between 1199 and 1210. It is believed that the same craftsmen were employed on this work who had been trained under William of Sens and William the Englishman at Canterbury, and Mr. Bond regarded it admiringly as "an Anglicised and improved version of the Canterbury quire, though still retaining traces of French influence, as in the square abacus and the foliated capitals of piers and shafts." The lateral nave chapels date chiefly from the later thirteenth century, and the Lady Chapel was lengthened by two bays and remodelled in three under Bishop Gilbert de S. Leophardi between 1288 and 1305. The first spire was raised over the central tower by Bishop Rede in *circa* 1380.

The west front, with its projecting Galilee, is flanked by rather gaunt Norman towers, of which the north is a recent imitation; and on the same side, standing detached a stone's throw away, is a plain *campanile*, with a turreted lantern storey, built during the fifteenth century to relieve the load on the central tower. The curvilinear window in the south transept is very fine, with a delightful small rose window in the gable above it; and the east end also has its rose window of plainer pattern above a trio of lancets flanked by pointed turrets. The simple central tower is surmounted by a tall spire, a competent rebuilding by Scott of the original, already repaired by Wren, which collapsed in 1861. The lateral chapels north and south of the nave form in effect a second pair

30 CHICHESTER : The Cathedral from the South

32 CHICHESTER : The Norman Nave looking East

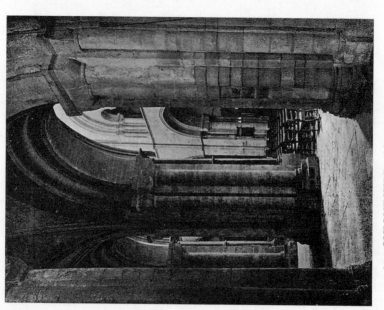

31 CHICHESTER : Norman Piers in the
North Nave Aisle

of aisles, as at Manchester; and the south side is largely screened by an irregularly shaped cloister, incorporating an arcade of Perpendicular tracery and a raftered wagon vault, intended as no more than a covered approach to the cathedral for the canons and vicars choral, and lacking a north walk. At the east end, the Lady

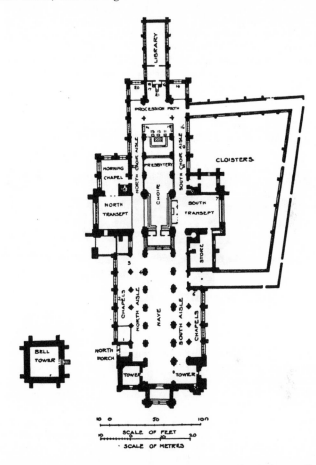

Chapel forms a long narrow extension lit by tall windows of varied Geometrical tracery.

On the interior, the nave is built to a close-knit Norman design (31, 32), which, if rather monotonous in the lower arcade, is relieved by the simple yet effective treatment of the triforium in coupled round-headed openings within larger containing arches —the four western bays with an interesting variety of incised diaper patterns in the spandrels. In contrast to its weight and dark-

F

ness, the bright vistas of the lateral aisle chapels, with their ample fenestration ranging from lancet to full Geometrical forms, are very pleasing. The quire continues the design of the nave, and built into the wall of its south aisle are two remarkable relief panels of Romanesque sculpture traditionally brought from Selsea, tinged with a strong Byzantine influence, representing Christ with Mary and Martha at Bethany (33), and the Raising of Lazarus. The range of quire fittings is modern with the exception of the stalls, unassuming work of the early sixteenth century, with some interesting misericords. East of the high altar screen, the Transitional presbytery is a graceful and striking design of two bays (34), individual in its grouping of four slender free-standing Purbeck

A MISERICORD

shafts around each main pier. The foliage carving of the capitals is advanced for its period (1199–1210), and the arches are round-headed, suggestive of Early English in their sharpness and depth of molding. The triforium design is of remarkable maturity, consisting of coupled lancets between clustered shafts of Purbeck within round containing arches, carved with foliage and figures in the tympana. An arch in the east wall gives access to the Lady Chapel, of which the three eastern bays were reconstructed *circa* 1290, terminating in a large Geometrical window, clumsily truncated by the vault. This latter is of two types, considerably more elaborate in the eastern bays; and in one compartment is a remnant of the beautiful floral arabesque painting executed by one Benardi in 1519 (who also worked on the quire vault), destroyed by order of the Chapter in 1817. The fine early-Perpendicular screen known as the Arundel Shrine, discarded from the quire during the last century, has been partially rebuilt in the *campanile*.

34 CHICHESTER: The Transitional Design of the Retro-Quire. A view from the South Triforium

33 CHICHESTER: Romanesque Relief, possibly from Selsea, in the South Quire Aisle. "Christ with Mary and Martha at Bethany"

35 DURHAM : The Norman Nave, with its varied pier designs, chevron arches and early ribbed vault. The screen is by Scott, and the distant rose window an insertion by Wyatt

36 DURHAM : The West End of the Nave, showing the splendid Font-Cover
installed after the Restoration by the famous High Church Bishop, Cosin

37 DURHAM : The Towers of the Cathedral rising above the Wooded Cliffs of the Wear

DURHAM

Durham is perhaps the best situated of all the English cathedrals; the familiar grouping of its towers above the wooded cliffs of the Wear (37) provides one of the most memorable views in England. But beyond the beauty of its surroundings, the church itself has a strong appeal: to the architect as the first example of ribbed stone vaulting on a grand scale, to the religious-minded as enshrining the names of Cuthbert and Bede, and to everyone for the romance of its origin and the stern dignity of its fabric. St. Cuthbert, whose early years were spent as a shepherd boy near Melrose, was a member of the evangelising brotherhood of Iona, and, between long periods of solitude, emerged first as prior, and later as unwilling bishop, of Lindisfarne, the Holy Island off the Northumberland coast from which the first conversion of Northern England was largely effected. Here he died and was buried in 687; but his remains were not left long undisturbed, for with the incursions of Danes and Norsemen and increasing insecurity of Northumbria, they were removed from Lindisfarne with the paraphernalia of the church, and launched on a remarkable period of over a hundred years of intermittent wandering. Each resting-place was commemorated by a church dedicated to the saint, and it was not until 997 that the brothers "with great Joy arrived with his Body at Dunholme," where, impressed by the strength of this rocky plateau surrounded on three sides by river, they raised a "little Church of Wands and Branches" on the site where the cathedral now stands. In 999 Aldhem completed the first stone church, where the shrine rested until 1093, when the second Norman bishop, William of St. Carileph, returning from exile on the death of Rufus, laid the foundations of a great new abbey church for the Benedictines, of which the eastern limb was ready by 1104. The nave was continued under Flambard, and the whole structure, including the stone vaults, finished in 1133. Thus, during a period of some forty years, every part of the cathedral was roofed with ribbed vaulting as the first master had planned it; and to sustain the thrust, the walls were strengthened with flying buttresses under the roof at the triforium level—the earliest and best form of this support.

In its massive strength and grandeur, the Anglo-Norman building that emerged remains unsurpassed of its type in England or outside it. Its plan, was typical of the Benedictine arrangement, and to-day the work of the Norman builders continues unaltered through the fabric, and is only replaced at the east end. The twin towers overlooking the cleft of the river are Norman to the clerestory level, and were raised to their present height during the thirteenth century. They 'compose' magnificently with the lofty splendour of the central tower, raised as late as 1474; and from the west, looking across the river and up steep dense slopes to the church, an impression of great height adds to their quiet dignity (37). Abutting on the west front is the remarkable 'Galilee,' placed as a kind of narthex screen-

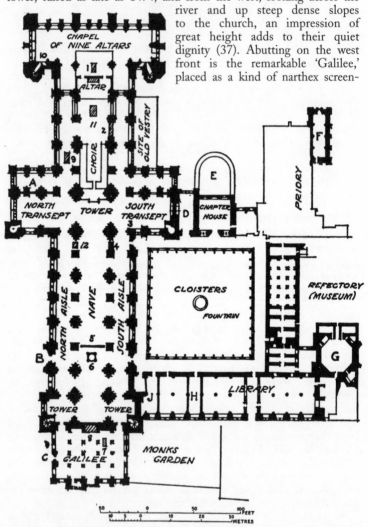

ing the entrance to the cathedral, added in 1175 as the gift of Hugh Pudsey, a nephew of King Stephen. It was built as the Lady Chapel, and is an exception to the almost invariable English rule that this should be placed east of the presbytery, the juxtaposition being due to the reputed intervention of St. Cuthbert, whose ineradicable aversion for women expressed itself in a number of structural failures when the work was begun in the usual position adjoining his shrine. As it stands, the building is an exquisite creation of the later twelfth century, divided into five aisles by arcades of rich chevron arches, with vistas comparable with the mosque of Cordoba (38). But though they produced a beautiful design, its architects, Richard and William, lacked the surveyor's skill, and the chapel had to be much strengthened under Bishop Langley to prevent it from sliding down the gorge and into the river.

The nave presents one of the finest Romanesque interiors in Europe (35), built with the quiet strength and dignity of superb proportions. The arcades were designed in pairs, the great transverse arches of the vault springing between each large compartment. These arches are pointed, and the photograph illustrates (35) how it was from this constructional use that the pointed fashion emerged. Massive cylindrical piers alternate with the clustered shafting of the main bays (4), the former decorated with a variety of bold simple chiselled diapers; and there is an effective use of the billet and chevron motives in the carving of the arch-molds and vaulting ribs. The same design continues through the transepts and quire, but in the latter, the easternmost bay was remodelled during the thirteenth century to form a transition to the transeptal Chapel of the Nine Altars at the extreme east end of the church, built to replace the original Norman apses. This work was begun under Prior Melsanly in 1242, following a threatened collapse, and the master-mason was Richard of Farnham, whose head, in a close-fitting cap, is carved on the wall-arcade. It was a happy idea—soon after to be borrowed with notable success for Fountains Abbey—and resulted in one of the most dignified and effective works of the thirteenth century (39). Here was lodged the shrine of St. Cuthbert; and if to-day the interior may seem rather empty and cold, the *Rites of Durham* provide a vivid picture of how it must have appeared in its prime, in all the gleam and glow of its colour decoration, with the famous tomb itself "exalted with the most curious workmanship, of fine and costly green marble, all limned and gilt with gold . . . the cover of the shrine being of wainscot . . . to which six very fine-sounding bells were fastened, which stirred all

THE CHAPEL OF THE NINE ALTARS: A TRIFORIUM VIEW

men's heart that were within the church to repair unto it. On either side of the said cover were painted four lively images, curiously wrought and miraculous to all beholders thereof. Also within the feretory on the north and south were almeries, varnished and finely painted and gilt over with fine little images, for the relics belonging to St. Cuthbert to lie in; all the costly reliques and jewels that hung about within the said feretory upon the irons, being accounted the most sumptuous and richest jewels in all this land."

Between the shrine and the high altar stood the great stone screen, still in existence, built in 1372–80 as the gift of John, Lord Neville, of Raby Castle. It is made of Dorset clunch, and was brought from London to Newcastle by sea. It contained 107 alabaster figures, with, in the centre, Our Lady accompanied by St. Cuthbert and St. Oswald, and the work is continued on either side of the sanctuary to form sedilia. On the south side of the quire stands the throne, made between 1545 and 1581 by order of Bishop Thomas Hatfield, to serve as his monument. It is worthy of the Palatine See and the Prince-Bishop who erected it, whose tomb, under an alabaster effigy, lies in an arch beneath. After the Civil War, the cathedral was used to confine Scottish prisoners taken at Dunbar in 1650, who destroyed the stalls. These were replaced soon after 1660 by Bishop Cosin of happy memory, whose gift survives, together with the towering font-cover at the west end (36), very delightful in its blending of medieval and Renaissance detail; but his great *pulpitum* was demolished by Scott, and a characteristic work substituted. The shrine of the Venerable Bede was in 1370 encased in plates of gold and silver and placed in the Lady Chapel, where his bones still lie under a plain tomb.

Durham suffered drastically at the hands of Wyatt, the first and therefore the least informed of the nineteenth-century restorers, who chiselled two inches off the fabric throughout, substituted a weak rose window at the east end, and was only barely prevented from pulling down the Galilee to make a carriage drive to the west front. Nevertheless the cathedral is fortunate in preserving the greater part of its monastic buildings, though the cloister has been considerably altered, and the fine apsed chapter-house adjoining the south transept shamefully treated by Wyatt, who tore down its east end to please the canons (who felt the cold and wanted a cosier room), and demolished the vault by knocking out the keystone and allowing the masonry to fall on the gravestones of the bishops, smashing them to pieces. It has since been rebuilt in something akin to its original form. The refectory was rebuilt in 1662–84 as a library; to the north-east is the octagonal prior's kitchen, ingenious-ly vaulted with a central louvre to emit the smoke, while the whole west walk is occupied by the dormitory, with an undercroft beneath, built under Bishop Skirlaw in 1398–1404. This room is 194 feet long and 41 feet wide, and is still ceiled with its original massive roof of oak trunks hardly touched by the axe. To-day it houses a priceless collection of Celtic crosses from the neighbourhood, with a number of old carved fragments from the cathedral.

39 DURHAM : Looking North in the Chapel of the Nine Altars, showing the original base of St Cuthbert's Shrine

38 DURHAM : The late-Norman Arcades of the Galilee

40 ELY : The Western Tower and Turrets

ELY

The ecclesiastical history of Ely begins in 673, when Etheldreda, princess of East Anglia, whose virginity had survived two marriages, founded a religious house on her own lands and on the site of the present cathedral. Etheldreda assigned her absolute principality of the so-called Isle of Ely to the new abbey, an endowment that formed the nucleus of the immense wealth that gradually accrued to it through the Middle Ages. Less than a hundred years later, in 870, the establishment was sacked and gutted by the Danes, and its religious put to the sword; but a handful of survivors escaped, creeping back a few years later to effect a partial restoration of the Saxon church, which was intermittently served by monks and deacons through the next century. In about 970, however, its rehabilitation was undertaken on a large scale, Benedictine monks were introduced, and new lands and revenues granted for the endowment. The conventual proprietorship of the Isle of Ely was confirmed by royal charter, and it is not surprising that with these powers, and in its commanding and isolated situation, the abbey grew to be one of the most opulent of the Middle Ages, like Durham the centre of a semi-independent 'County Palatine' that continued to be ruled until comparatively recent times by its own Prince-Bishops.

The building of the present cathedral was begun about 1080 under Abbot Simeon, starting contrary to custom with the transepts. Despite the long resistance of Hereward, and his last stand at the 'Camp of Refuge' near Ely, which has become a national legend, the fabric of the Saxon church had suffered little or no damage at the hands of the Normans, and its reconstruction on such a scale can only be attributed to the building urge of the period, which demanded ever larger and more magnificent churches to the glory of God and the enhanced prestige of the Benedictines. The work was suspended during the troubled reign of Rufus, but by 1106 the eastern limb was completed, and the remains of the canonised foundress, with those of her pious companions Sexburga, Ermenilda and Withburga, ceremonially reinterred before the high altar. The building of the nave, with the reconstruction of the monastic quarters, was continued gradually through the twelfth century; during the episcopacy of Bishop Riddell (1174–1189), we read that "he carried on the new work, and the Tower and the West End of the Church, almost to the top." The next stage was added to the west front under Bishop Northwold between 1229 and 1254, but the beautiful projecting Galilee porch, one of the flowers of

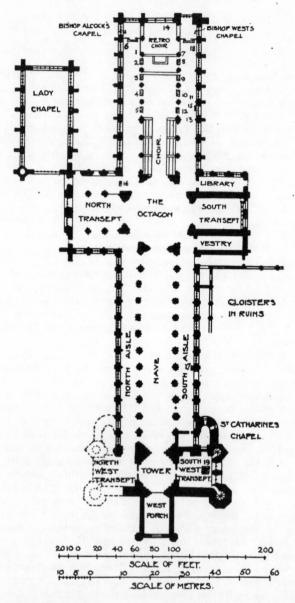

thirteenth-century building, was probably constructed at a slightly earlier date under Bishop Eustace. Northwold's episcopacy also saw the demolition of part of the old Norman quire, and the building of the present presbytery; and from the completion of the latter, no work on a large scale was undertaken on the cathedral until 1322, when, on the night of February 12th, the central tower collapsed, destroying three entire bays of the eastern limb. It was this event that presented the sub-prior and later sacrist, Alan of Walsingham, with his immense opportunity. As custodian of the fabric, his office was that of general organiser and clerk of the works for a tremendous programme of building, and though it would be rash to credit him with either the design or the engineering of the splendid octagonal lantern built to replace the tower (42), it is certain that his energy and organising capacity immeasurably aided its realisation in terms of stone and timber, while the three western bays of the quire and the beautiful Lady Chapel, in itself a spring-time of fourteenth-century carving, were also completed under his supervision.

Ely to-day, on its mound of firmer soil looking out over the expanse of the Fens, has a rather abstracted and sleepy air—with the exception of Wells the smallest episcopal city in England, though its spacious parish church of St. Mary and the beautiful and distinctive old houses of the close are full of interest. The red-brick Tudor Bishop's Palace adjoins the cathedral, and the precincts are entered through a magnificent stone gatehouse, the so-called 'Ely Porta,' built under Prior Buckton in the four-teenth century. At close range, the open green in front of the cathedral adds much to the effect of the west front—despite the loss of its north transept, one of the most striking compositions of its type in England. The most beautiful of all the views of the cath-edral, however, is approaching it across the fenland from the south or east, when in good weather its tall western tower and long roof-line stand out for miles in silhouette above a flat, uniform and practically featureless landscape (41).

The tier upon tier of close-knit arcading that pattern the faces of this tower show a gradual process of development from sim-ple Romanesque to full-formed lancet type (40). It was completed during the fourteenth century by the addition of a lofty lantern storey, flanked by octagonal turrets; and the single surviving transept also terminates in twin polygonal turrets, that rise to almost double its height. The disappearance of the north-west transept remains a mystery, but its original existence is corroborated by the carving of one of the fourteenth-century corbels of the octagon, showing St. Etheldreda holding the model of a church with two western transepts, which obviously represents Ely. Completed with both transepts and crowned with spires, the design must have been one of the most spectacular in earlier medieval building, a possible effect of flatness being counteracted by the building out of the tall arcaded 'Galilee,' with its open-traceried outer doorway and fine sculptured entrance to the cathedral.

The elevations of the nave represent a plain and unambitious

Norman fabric, of which the two lower ranges of windows are later insertions; and here on the south side is the small Romanesque Prior's Door, with its rich carving in the tympanum. Later windows have also been placed in the gables of both transepts, and adjoining that of the north is the detached fourteenth-century Lady Chapel (42), now a parish church, lovely and complete in itself, with its ranges of crocketed pinnacles and great areas of traceried glass. The eastern limb is an undistinctive thirteenth-century design that has suffered considerable adaptation, only two bays on the south side retaining the original triforium of Bishop Northwold, which it is interesting

THE ROMANESQUE CARVING OF THE PRIOR'S DOOR

to compare with the higher and later reconstruction that survives. Alan of Walsingham's Octagon over the crossing (42) is nowadays perhaps best seen from a distance, when its pristine purity of outline can still be appreciated despite the frippery of crockets and pinnacles added of recent years. Very beautiful are the great curvilinear windows that show their traceried heads at the diagnonal corners, and the crowning lights of the wooden lantern are well-proportioned and stately, though its parapets and turrets have a suspiciously smartened air.

The Norman nave is one of the finest in England (43, 44), and also one of the latest, for it was not finally completed until the latter part of the twelfth century. Like Peterborough, it represents the last phase of Romanesque in England, but the coming transition

41 ELY : The Profile of the Cathedral from the South

42 ELY : The Octagon, with the Lady Chapel and North Transept

43 ELY : The Nave and Octagon, looking East

44 ELY : Looking Westward down the Nave from the Octagon

45 ELY : The Fourteenth-Century Lady Chapel, with its rich
broken wall-arcading

46 ELY : The Interior of Bishop Alcock's riotous little
Chantry of 1488 at the East End

is evident in the slenderness of the arcading shafts of the triforium and clerestory, and the substitution of well-proportioned moldings for carved ornament in the arches. As at Norwich, the unusual height of the triforium and the insertion of later windows produce an unusually full even lighting of the interior, but looking upwards, the dignity of the effect is diminished by the canted wooden ceiling jammed down incongruously like a lid over the clerestory, hardly improved in itself by the mid-nineteenth-century paintings of Messrs. Styleman Le Strange and Gambier Parry. The nave terminates westward in a tremendous Perpendicular arch—a recasing of the original Norman work to strengthen the tower; and the south-west transept is used as a baptistery, to which the little apsed chapel of St. Catherine forms an annex, a scholarly reconstruction by Willis of about 1860.

The transepts are lofty and well-lighted, and are the only portion of any major English cathedral to carry open hammerbeam roofs, which are effective in their design and recolouring. At the crossing, Alan of Walsingham's Octagon remains the most daring and original architectural conception of the English Middle Ages (41–44). Four lofty arches carried on clustered piers rise to the full roof height of nave, quire and transepts (43), and the diagonal sides between them are occupied by tall windows of flowing curvilinear tracery, above canopied niches and ground arches corresponding with the quire arcade. From the capitals of the main piers spring eight segments of timber vaulting, the spreading ribs of which are yoked by an octagonal collar, from which rises the slender upper lantern, with its tall ring of windows. In the present age of steel and concrete, such an undertaking would certainly tax the engineer's ability; its realisation in timber during the Middle Ages was a structural achievement of the first magnitude, and it is not surprising to find that twelve years were needed for its completion. The length and breadth of England was ransacked for oaks of sufficient scantling—it would be ransacked in vain nowadays, for the invisible supporting beams are 63 feet long and approximately 3 feet square, and the roads and bridges into Ely had to be strengthened for their transportation. To-day, despite the efforts of Victorian decorators and the lurid nightmare of its glass, the Ely Octagon remains a work of fascinating loveliness and precision, and its lighting effect is unforgettable, forming a luminous pool in the centre of the church that contrasts with the deep chiaroscuro of the arcades.

Scott's characteristic screen requires no comment, and beyond it, the first three bays of the quire are occupied by the fourteenth-century reconstruction necessitated by the collapse of the tower—florid spectacular work of about 1340, with a lavish use of cusping and rosettes. It is crowned by a delightful lierne vault—an innovation in a church of timber ceilings—and though the design has come in for considerable praise and criticism, it is not easy to pass a considered judgment on its character, for the main arcades are almost entirely concealed by the fine though modernised stalls, and an ungainly bedizened organ sprawls over the north triforium. The six remaining bays of the presbytery were built under Bishop Northwold about 1240 to an effective and well-proportioned design, of which the influence is apparent in the later and more sumptuous 'Angel Choir' at Lincoln. The two small chapels that form the eastern aisle extremities are among the most interesting and riotous expressions of waning English Gothic. Of these, Bishop Alcock's chantry to the north (46) dates from 1488, and in its elaborate confusion of canopy-work and carving is reminiscent of the final phase of Gothic in France, as in the Savoy mausoleum at Brou-en-Bresse. It is perhaps unfair, however, to judge it without its innumerable statues, smashed after the Reformation; and this also applies to Bishop West's Chapel on the south side, though here the work, dating from 1534, has an almost lace-like delicacy that is far more consistent with Perpendicular practice. The magnificent panelled ceiling, described by Celia Fiennes as "One Entire stone most delicately Carv'd in great Poynts," is definitely Renaissance in treatment, as is the arabesque panel over the entrance, with its beautiful wrought-iron gateway. The Lady Chapel (1321–1349) adjoining the north transept was built as a spacious aisleless hall, with immense curvilinear windows to east and west (45), its forty-foot breadth spanned by a lierne vault. Beautiful as the interior is to-day, its appearance before the demolition of its forest of statues must have been unforgettable, and the mason-craft of its canopy-work and wall-arcading, though sadly mutilated, remains one of the most glorious displays of English naturalistic carving. The cloister was destroyed after the Reformation, but a section of the arcade of the monastic infirmary remains curiously embedded in the fronts of later buildings in the close. Other fragments of the monastic ranges are incorporated in schools and houses, and fortunately the charming little fourteenth-century chapel of Prior Crauden remains intact, and is used as the chapel of King's School.

PRIOR CRAUDEN'S CHAPEL IN THE CLOSE

EXETER

When in 1050 the see of Devon and Cornwall was transferred from Crediton to Exeter under Bishop Leofric, the abbey church of St. Mary and St. Peter was adopted as the new cathe- dral, a building of some pre- ten- sions for its period which sufficed until the advent of the first Norman bishop, Warelast, a nephew of the Conqueror and later chaplain to both Rufus and Henry I. A larger structure was then begun further west, of which only the present transept towers survive; and this had done service for less than eighty years when, in *circa* 1260, Walter Brons- combe, the first of a famous line of building bishops, with whom the work of enlarg- ing and adorning the cathe- dral was generally nearer a passion than a duty, began the eastward ex- tension of the presbytery on the site of the original Saxon church, together with a Lady Chapel in the fash- ion of the time. With the excep- tion of this exten- sion, the Norman plan was followed throughout the ensuing re-construction, the height of the towers, which were re-tained as transepts and are thus unique in England save at the daugh- ter church of Ottery St. Mary, regulating the scale

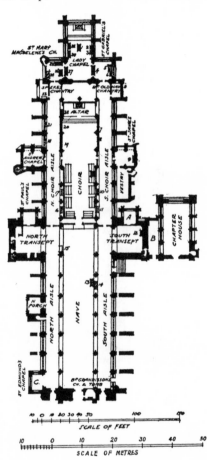

throughout. Bronscombe's work embraced the eastern chapels and the Lady Chapel to the cill level. Peter Quivil (1280–1291) continued it, and adapted the towers as transepts, and under Thomas Bytton (1292–1307), the presbytery was completed with its aisles, and the

H

39

Norman quire remodelled. Walter Stapledon, who followed him (1308–1326), furnished this quire largely out of his own pocket. A chaplain to Pope Clement V, Lord Treasurer of England and one of the first courtiers of his period, he did much to create in the cathedral that "radiantly decorative" character that is still its very individual charm, and the fine screen, bishop's throne and rich sedilia date from his epis-

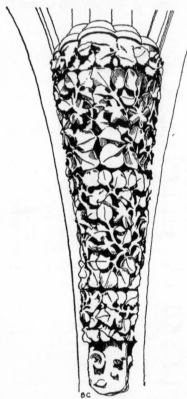

copate. He was murdered by the mob, defending London for Edward II, but his successor, John Grandisson (1327–1369), continued the work with unabated enthusiasm, and under him the nave was completed and the whole vaulted. By the close of the fourteenth century, Exeter was one of the most sumptuously appointed of the English cathedrals, possessed of a rare and dazzling consistence in its "luxurious spendthrift art" that has happily to a great extent been preserved through the vicissitudes of its later history.

Built of grey stone in a red sandstone country, the cathedral fabric, with the sole exception of the towers, represents a steady and continuous growth from the close of the thirteenth and throughout the fourteenth century, and is the finest surviving work of that most intriguing period. The plan is symmetrical throughout, chapel to chapel, tower to tower, window to window; and the design has a real exuberance and sunny charm in its display of tall pinnacles, striding buttresses and ranges of broad, splayed windows, with an imaginative diversity of Geometrical tracery that makes each a new excitement (47). The west front is built in three planes, with a curved triangular window in the gable and a vast lovely window of complex tracery filling most of the upper wall (48). The entrance screen (49) dates from the last quarter of the fourteenth century, and displays in three tiers an array of kings, popular saints

CARVED CORBEL IN THE NAVE

47 EXETER : A South-East View of the Cathedral from the Palace Garden, showing the Lady Chapel, Quire, and South Transept Tower

48   EXETER : The Cathedral by Night. A Floodlit View of the West Front

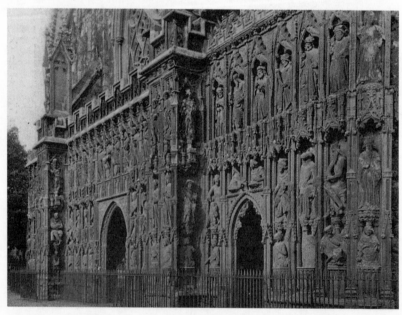

49   EXETER : The Sculptured Screen of the West Front

50 EXETER : The Quire, looking to the East Window. In the right
foreground is a section of the fourteenth-century Bishop's Throne

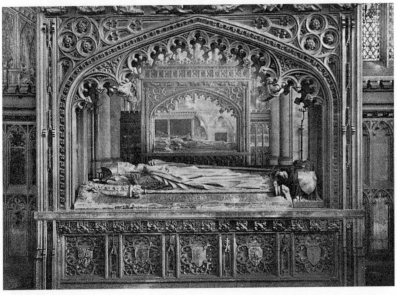

51 EXETER : The Canopied Tombs of Bishops Bronscombe and Stafford,
matching one another, with typical Exeter regularity, across the Retro-quire

52   EXETER : The Cathedral Vista from the Nave, showing the level stream of the Vault from West to East and Bishop Stapledon's *Pulpitum* adapted to a later use

and angels under canopies, much damaged, largely as a result of the annual Guy Fawkes bonfires held for centuries outside the church, and now considerably renewed.

In spite of its moderate dimensions, the interior gives an impression of peculiar spaciousness, enhanced by the consistent excellence of the proportions, the beauty of the lighting and the long uninterrupted stream of the vault through nave and quire (52). The piers, with their unusual stone seating around the bases, are built of massive blocks of unpolished Purbeck marble, sharply and exquisitely molded into a multiplicity of shafts (7), their soft bluegrey colouring contrasting with the yellow sandstone of the arcade and the white Caen freestone of the tri-forium and clerestory. The low band of the triforium consists of a blind arcade of small cusped arches, grouped four to a bay, surmounted by an elegant pierced parapet of a double range of quatrefoils (7). Above this rise the spacious windows of the clerestory, and over all, the splendid vault springs from slender shafts that descend low to the crisply molded capitals of the piers, ter-minating in

CARVED BOSS, "THE MURDER OF BECKET," IN THE NAVE VAULT

beautiful tapering corbels of massed foliage, with occasional figures, that incorporate some of the finest carving in the cathedral. The ridge line has a series of carved bosses, the finest of which are in the quire, with subjects such as the Crucifixion and Murder of Becket alternating with the foliations beloved of the Exeter craftsmen.

The presbytery (50) is the noblest part of the building, dating from the close of the thirteenth century when the style, unshackled from outworn precedent, blossomed into a short Spring of loveliness that was soon again to lose its freshness in a new subjection. The proportions, moldings and carvings are as nearly perfect as is possible to the human mind, the only comparable work of the same period being the chapter-house at Southwell Minster (103, 104). The preservation of the Fabric Rolls allows us to follow the construction step by step, and learn something of the men responsible for the achievement. The carver of all this beauty of corbel and boss was William of Montacute, from just over the border in Somerset; his portrait can be seen under the figure of St. Catherine on one of the corbels. The quire fortunately retains much of its original furniture, including the bishop's throne (50), 57 feet high and incorporating some of the finest woodcarving in England, which, together with the stalls at Winchester and Lancaster and the sedilia at Beverley, forms our criterion of fourteenth-century carpentry. Up to the close of this period the carpenter followed the mason's ideals—the work, when coloured and gilt, might easily be taken for stone—just as later the stonemason copied the carpenter in his slender pinnacled creations. Master Thomas de Winton, who was responsible for the stalls at Winchester, came to Exeter to choose the timber for the new throne, and no doubt provided the design. He was paid 3s. a week for four weeks, and 5s. for his journey home. The head carpenter, Robert de Galmeton, was paid 2s. 6d. a week, and the head carver, Walter of Membury, 2s. 9d. —both Devon men. The throne was finally set up in 1312, and the great reredos, since destroyed, with its fifty statues and silver dorsal, the tall sedilia and the *pulpitum* (52) followed shortly after. The latter is only in part preserved, the solid wall on the quire side having been broken through, though Scott, to his credit, managed to save the whole from demolition. The gallery of panels above originally contained sculpture (the Roll for 1322–1323 mentions "45 images for 11 panels, with a Doom"), and the present paintings that take its place are of the Stuart period. At the time of the Commonwealth, a wall was erected at the crossing by the Puritans, dividing the cathedral into two preaching churches, the "East" and "West Peters." The credit for its removal belongs to Bishop Seth Ward of happy memory, who after the Restoration laid down some £25,000 on necessary repairs and renovations.

The building of the nave was interrupted by the Black Death, and when the pestilence had abated, no glaziers could be found for the windows, which had to be made up with wattle and daub. When work was resumed on the vault and the windows reopened, a great net, extending from roof to floor, was bought to keep pigeons out of the quire. The piers were worked at the Purbeck quarries at Corfe by the Canons, father and son, and shipped by sea, thence up the Exe to Topsham. The beautiful minstrels' gallery in the north triforium (7) was built for the Palm Sunday services, and is faced with niches containing angels playing musical instruments. The great window of the west end is of nine lights, incorporating in its head a splendid circle (48); its eighteenth-century glass by William Peckett of York was replaced in 1904, but some fragments by this craftsman survive in the portion of the cloister reconstructed by Pearson. In the transepts, the elegant corbelled galleries were added under Quivil to complete a continuous triforium passage around the building; and in the north is the great astronomical clock—a type of mechanical device for which the West Country was famous during the Middle Ages.

Throughout the cathedral, the chapels and chantries form a splendid series, with their beautiful late screens of wood and stone, and the sepulchral work is particularly notable, including effigies of the bishops from Bartholomew in 1184 to Cotton in 1621. Sometimes these tombs are matched, with typical Exeter regularity, across the church, as with Bishops Bronscombe and Stafford in the presbytery, under canopies added in the fifteenth century (51), and the rich sixteenth-century chantries of Bishop Oldham and Sir John Speke. A curious little chapel dedicated to St. Radegunde, and built in the thickness of the wall of the west front, contained the tomb of Bishop Grandisson, but was sacked during the reign of Elizabeth. The rectangular chapter-house adjoining the south transept was built in the thirteenth century and largely remodelled in the fifteenth, when the large windows were inserted. The disused Bishop's Palace, of which the garden envelops the east end (47), contains a thirteenth-century chapel 'improved' by Butterfield, and a pleasant Tudor fragment.

AN AERIAL VIEW FROM THE SOUTH EAST

I

GLOUCESTER

THE CATHEDRAL CHURCH OF ST. PETER

The first abbey dedicated to St. Peter at Gloucester was founded by Osric, viceroy of King Ethelred, in 681, whose sister Kyneburga was appointed abbess of a dual foundation of monks and nuns. In 832 the church was rebuilt in stone, and secular priests installed in place of the religious, but in 1022 Canute, in the words of Leland, "for ill lyvinge expellyd secular clerks, and by the counsell of Wolstane, Bysshope of Wurcester, bringethe in monkes." These monks were of the Benedictine Order, and their unpopularity was to some extent justified by the laxity of their morals and discipline. In 1058, however, the monastery was taken in hand by Aldred, Bishop of Worcester, who rebuilt the church on a larger scale from the foundations; and in 1072, on the death of the Saxon abbot, a Norman monk, Serlo, was appointed in his place, who found the establishment shrunk to a *personnel* of only two monks and eight novices. Serlo, with his energy and ability, brought new life to the declining foundation, and within a few years had so increased the number of the monks that rebuilding was again considered necessary. The present church was begun in 1089, only thirty-one years after the completion of Aldred's entirely new building, and was consecrated in 1100 by a concourse of bishops.

It is uncertain how much of the cathedral was completed at the time of the consecration, but the fabric records of the next two hundred years show little more than a catalogue of minor alterations and additions. It was after the accession of Wygmore (1329–1337) to the abbot's office that the second important phase began in the evolution of the building as we know it to-day. The murder of Edward II at Berkeley Castle in 1327 in the popular imagination transformed a weak neurotic king into the character of a saint and martyr. After his death, the body had been timidly refused by the abbeys of Bristol, Kingswood and Malmesbury, but Abbot Thokey, with commendable loyalty to a sovereign he had more than once entertained at Gloucester, "fetched him from Berkeley Castle in his own chariot, sumptuously adorned and painted with the arms of our monastery, and brought him to Gloucester, where all the convent received him honourably in their solemn robes, with a procession of the whole city, and buried him in our church, in the north aisle, hard by the high altar." The miracle-working reputation of the relics brought a crowd of pilgrims to Gloucester, and with them funds for the reconstitution of the quire and transepts as a splendid mortuary chapel to the profitable saint. Wygmore was a man of taste and discrimination, and his choice of the "clever and rather eccentric artists" of the Severn school to carry out a scheme

53 GLOUCESTER : The Cathedral from the South-East, showing the almost detached Lady Chapel and the tall lantern of the Quire Clerestory raised high above the Norman fabric of the Aisles

54 GLOUCESTER : The Reconstructed Quire, facing to the Vast Canted
Window of the East End

55 GLOUCESTER : The Lady Chapel, looking West to the Gallery-Bridge
connecting it with the Quire Triforium

56 GLOUCESTER : The North Walk of the Fan-Vaulted Cloisters,
showing the Carrels, or Study-Niches, of the Monks' *Scriptorium*

of decorative panelling in the soft white local stone of Cheltenham resulted not only in one of the most lovely and original works of English later-Gothic (8, 54), but in an architectural revolution of which the influence was persistent through the next two hundred years. The central tower (53) was begun under Abbot Seabroke (1450–1457), and before it was completed the present Lady Chapel was added in 1500, to replace a thirteenth-century building that was demolished. The nineteenth century saw an irritating restoration by Sir Gilbert Scott, in which some of the delightful Renaissance fittings shown by Britton vanished.

To-day, the cathedral stands pleasantly in a close of old houses, but there are few good views of it from the city, and the best are to be had from the low green water-meadows of the Severn, where the tall central tower and clerestory appear splendidly conspicuous in the distance above a vista of roofs. Similarly, at close range, it is this rich Perpendicular tower, 225 feet high, that largely dominates the composition (53), rising in tiers of crocketed canopies to a crowning storey of open stonework, with four lofty pinnacles connected by a pierced parapet. The principal ranges of the cathedral, nave, quire and Lady Chapel form an uneven roof-line of three levels, and, save for the projecting fifteenth-century south porch, the nave is fairly plain in elevation, with even ranges of large windows that include, in the south aisle, the ball-flower fenestration of Abbot Thokey's building. Despite the insertion of fourteenth-century windows, the transepts, with their tall arcaded turrets, remain largely Norman in fabric, as are the quire aisles, with their clustering segmental chapels, though here also are later windows deep-cut in the thick early walls (53). Above these latter rise the tall windows of the Perpendicular clerestory, surmounted by a skeleton parapet rising at the east end to a lofty openwork gable flanked by turrets. Complete in itself, the Lady Chapel stands a little apart to the east, connected with the cathedral by an ambulatory bridge, beautiful and stately in its even spacious fenestration (53), and typical of the hall churches and college chapels of its period (*circa* 1500).

The Norman nave of seven bays (57) is a fine giant of the same west-country type as Tewkesbury and Pershore, consisting of an arcade of smooth cylindrical piers, 30 feet high to the plainly molded capitals, narrowly spaced and carrying ranges of rather meagre round-headed arches, well and plainly molded with the billet on the outer face. The triforium is rather insignificant, consisting of a blind coupled arcade of four small arches to each bay, flanked on either hand by the clustered Purbeck shafts of the thirteenth-century vault—built by the monks' own hands, and rather clumsily at that, for its low springing results in a bad misfit that divides the clerestory windows into isolated compartments, improving neither the lighting nor the symmetry. The north aisle is roofed with a plain Norman ribbed vault, but in the south, the vault was reconstructed early in the fourteenth century (58), and here also are the remarkable ball-flower windows added under Abbot Thokey. The two western bays were rebuilt with the west front in about 1430, following the demolition of the Norman towers, under Abbot Morwent, who probably intended

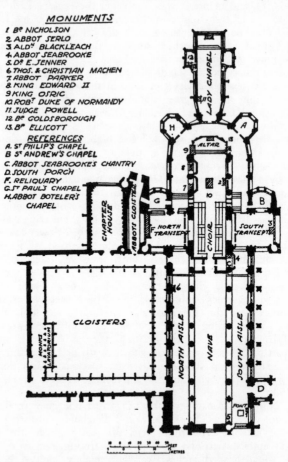

MONUMENTS

1 Bᵖ NICHOLSON
2 ABBOT SERLO
3 ALDⁿ BLACKLEACH
4 ABBOT SEABROOKE
5 Dᵖ E. JENNER
6 THOS. & CHRISTIAN MACHEN
7 ABBOT PARKER
8 KING EDWARD II
9 KING OSRIC
10 ROBᵗ DUKE OF NORMANDY
11 JUDGE POWELL
12 Bᵖ GOLDSBOROUGH
13 Bᵖ ELLICOTT

REFERENCES

A. St PHILIP'S CHAPEL
B St ANDREW'S CHAPEL
C. ABBOT SEABROOKES CHANTRY
D. SOUTH PORCH
F. RELIQUARY
G. St PAUL'S CHAPEL
H. ABBOT BOTELER'S CHAPEL

to reconstruct the entire nave after this plain Perpendicular model. An eighteenth-century scheme to transform its appearance by fluting the Norman piers, originating from no less a person than William Kent, was also happily thwarted; but it is pleasant to find that some of the dark oak fittings of *circa* 1680 have been preserved, contrasting in their sober Anglicanism with the florid Victorian outburst of Clayton and Bell in the windows.

At the eastern ends of the aisles, the delicate attenuated transformation of Abbot Wygmore appears in utter contrast to the smooth solidity of the Norman nave (58). As has been seen, its conception has been traced to the ingenious school of Severn masons, which, during the earlier fourteenth century, produced such exciting structural novelties as the open-arch vaulting in their own cathedral (19), and the great cage of inverted arches enclosing the crossing at Wells (110). In the Gloucester quire, their experiments are crystallised in a new style of surface decoration, a style of light skeleton panelling and vast transomed windows of many lights, with slender molded mullions carried vertically to their heads (8, 54). The casing of the sombre Romanesque design was effected with a dexterous economy of both material and labour that especially compels modern admiration; and as a scheme of decoration, it remained unsurpassed in the two hundred years' output of the so-called Perpendicular manner which it engendered.

The transepts were included in the reconditioning. Here large new windows were inserted in the ends, and the arms roofed with complex ramifying lierne vaults, that in the south transept skilfully mitred without bosses. In the north, the thirteenth-century reliquary, with its Purbeck shafting and plate tracery, strikes an oddly discordant note. A curious effect results from the appearance across the aisle-ends of the great internal flying buttresses that support the tower (58); and at the crossing, the main arches of the transepts are spanned by graceful 'flying arches' of light masonry which carry the springing of the vault above the central space. From here, the view eastward up the quire is of an unforgettable beauty. In its delicate yet insistent verticality, its spaciousness and brilliant lighting, the design is the prototype of the utterly national Perpendicular hall church (54), rising in the clerestory to a continuous range of windows that forms in effect an immense single lantern (53), and terminating eastward in a vast expanse of glass that fills the entire end of the building. This window is curiously canted in three planes to give greater area, and contains much original glass. The crowning member is the lofty lierne vault, which, if a little tedious in its complexity, has a fine profusion of sculptured bosses, including over the high altar an adorable group of carved angels playing on instruments, one of which is reproduced in Fig. 2. The stalls, though considerably restored, form a remarkable achievement for their period (*circa* 1380), with niche-like canopies and a brilliant series of misericords. The shrine of Edward II remains intact in the north arcade (8), its profuse attenuated canopy-work contrasting with the calm dignity of the effigy, one of the earliest examples of alabaster carving in England. It is curious to compare this work with the stiff sword-drawing effigy of Robert of Normandy which has been moved into the centre of the quire (8), and still retains much of its colouring.

In the reconstruction of the quire, the Norman aisles were left intact, roofed with heavy groined vaults, and at the east end

K

forming a spacious curved ambulatory around the church. To this
the triforium passage forms a second storey, its broad arcade
patterned by the slender vertical shafts and transoms of the Perpendicular scaffolding. It is roofed with a plain *demi-berceau*, or
half-barrel vault, and completing the connection around the east
end is a curious little Norman passage built out from the church
and called the 'whispering gallery,' from its remarkable acoustic
properties. This passage passes over the vestibule that connects
the Lady Chapel with the cathedral, and from this virtual bridge (55)
a splendid interior view is obtained of the interior of that lovely little
building, conceived on almost identical lines to the quire, though
completed over a century and a half later, and to all intents and purposes walled with panelled glass. The east window is of nine lights,
retaining some fragments of its old glass, and facing it at the west
end of the chapel, the vaulted vestibule is surmounted by a magnificent open screen of Perpendicular tracery. Over all is an elaborate
lierne vault, very similar to that of the quire and profuse in sculptured bosses. The two miniature transepts reveal beautiful little
chantry chapels, with open musicians' galleries in their upper
storeys.

The cloisters are the finest and best preserved in England, and
their glory is the magnificent fan vault that is continuous around
all four walks (56), probably the earliest of its type to be constructed. The *scriptorium* in the south wall is almost as it was left
by the monks, with twenty small compartments, or carrels, for the
desks of the writers, and in the north walk is the most complete
surviving *lavatorium* for the monks' ablutions, still preserving its
stone towel cupboard. The cloister is glazed with opaque modern
glass, and the garth has been appropriated as the deanery garden,
so that the fine view from it of the cathedral is no longer available to the public. On the east side is the rectangular Norman
chapter-house, roofed with a pointed barrel-vault, and lit by a
large Perpendicular window inserted in the east end. Between this
and the north transept is the vaulted Norman slype, called the
Abbots' Cloister, forming the undercroft of a later library. A second
passage out of the cloister at the north-west corner leads to the
ruined arcade of the infirmary, and a delightful miniature cloister
enclosing what was probably the 'farmery garth,' or herb-garden
for the brewing of medicines.

ACROSS THE SEVERN VALLEY FROM THE NORTH-WEST

58 GLOUCESTER : A Glimpse of Perpendicular from the South Aisle of the Nave

57 GLOUCESTER : Norman Piers in the Nave

60 HEREFORD: A North-West View of the Cathedral, showing the Central Tower, North Transept, and Bishop Beckington's Porch

59 HEREFORD: A Glimpse of the Nave from the South Aisle

HEREFORD

The cathedral lies pleasantly on its green in a busy country town, and its burly tower forms the central feature of some attractive views across the Wye. The first church is said to have been raised about 825 above the tomb of Ethelred, King of the East Angles, decoyed to his death by the great Offa of Mercia; and of the twelfth-century building of Robert de Losinga which replaced it, the archaic east wall of the south transept is possibly the sole remaining fragment. The main nave design and reconstructed quire date from *circa* 1110–1145, but the course of later work on the retro-quire under Bishop William de Vere (1186–1199) is something of a puzzle, though it is certain that the Lady Chapel that lies east of it was practically completed by 1220. Some fifty years later, the north transept was partially rebuilt to a striking design, probably under Bishop Aquablanca, who lies in it. Thomas de Cantilupe, who succeeded to the see in 1275, was one of the most powerful and dignified prelates of the thirteenth century, whose long spell of office as Chancellor of England had ended with the fall of Montfort. He died in Rome, where he had journeyed to settle a rankling dispute with Canterbury, and here his body was rather gruesomely boiled down by his chaplain, Swinfield, who followed him as bishop, and the bones brought back to Hereford to form the nucleus of a promising shrine. Swinfield made numerous additions to the cathedral that probably included the nave aisles and small eastern transepts, and his successor, Orleton, another famous politician-bishop, rebuilt the central tower *circa* 1316, with a timber spire that has disappeared. From 1786 onwards, some £70,000 has been expended on three major restorations, apart from minor patching, with results that aesthetically are to be deplored, though there is no doubt that, as was so often the case during the nineteenth century, a quite remarkable engineering work was accomplished that almost certainly saved the central tower.

On the exterior, this broad rich tower (60) is easily the most impressive feature, its worn sandstone encrusted with innumerable crumbling ball-flowers. Bishop Booth's two-storeyed north porch (60) is a distinguished late-Perpendicular addition of *circa* 1530, curiously superimposed over Swinfield's earlier work, and somewhat reminiscent in design of that at Peterborough. The collapse in 1786 of the single central tower of the original west front opened the way for a series of ravaging reconstructions over a period of eighty years. Wyatt's lean design has not long been replaced by the work of J. Oldrid Scott, while at the east end, the Lady Chapel, heavily handled by Cottingham, has something of the appearance of a recent school chapel. On the interior, the most consistent piece of old work is the Norman nave arcade, with its massive cylindrical piers, shallow capitals carved with intricate interlacements, and well-molded arches (59). The triforium and clerestory are a weak redesigning by Wyatt, who shortened the whole by one bay; and the vault is an imitation in painted wood.

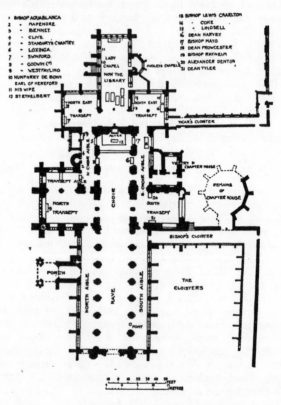

It is difficult to write adequately of the tortured 'art metalwork' of the quire screen installed by Scott. To its making went 11,200 lb. of iron, 5,000 lb. of copper and brass, 50,000 pieces of mosaic and 300 cut stones. The result, slightly ravaged by over half a century's wear, tear and oxidisation, is a melancholy commentary on the transience of even the most eminent taste.

The transepts represent the greatest patchwork of the fabric. The northern arm has its east wall built to Bishop Aquablanca's remarkable design of *circa* 1270, in which the arches are practically triangular-headed, with triple-pierced quatrefoils in the triforium tympana, and rich diapering in the spandrels. The exceedingly tall slender windows of Geometrical tracery are delightful, of a type seldom found in England outside this district. The pedestal of the shrine of St. Thomas Cantilupe has been removed to this transept, richly arcaded with Purbeck shafting, having in the lower panels fifteen carved figures of Knights Templars, of which Order the canonised bishop was a former grand master. The east wall of the south arm is of the early Norman design of Bishop Robert's eleventh-century church, though the entire transept was vaulted and generally reconstituted in Perpendicular times. The rather gloomy quire is of a Norman design that recalls the nave, though with compound piers and a tremendously massive triforium, terminating eastward in an arch through which can be seen the central vaulting pier of the Lady Chapel vestibule, its upper spandrel loaded with Cottingham's indifferent sculpture, replacing as a background to the high altar Bishop Bisse's preposterous 'Grecian' screen removed in 1841. The stalls are original work of the fifteenth century, with openwork ogee canopies of a curious 'beak' type.

THE NORTH WINDOWS OF THE LADY CHAPEL

The small eastern transepts form a single composition with the retro-quire, each with a central octagonal pier to carry the vaulting; and the low but quite spacious eastern Lady Chapel is a thirteenth-century design, of which the most distinctive feature is the deep recessing of the lancet windows with five orders of slender shafts, though the eastern wall is a rebuilding. Off the south side opens the beautiful two-storeyed Perpendicular chantry of Bishop Audley, richly panelled and fan-vaulted, with a little gallery overlooking the chapel. Only two walks remain of the Bishops' Cloister, with its elaborate tracery design; of what has vanished, much of the stone was used, with that of the chapter-house, to repair the houses of post-Reformation bishops. The unobtrusive Vicars' Cloister retains an old walk, with some richly carved roof-timbering, and the famous chained library should certainly be visited.

LICHFIELD

What must have been one of the loveliest of the smaller cathedrals stands on high ground on the edge of a quiet little Midland town, and its immediate surroundings are very beautiful, its trio of spires

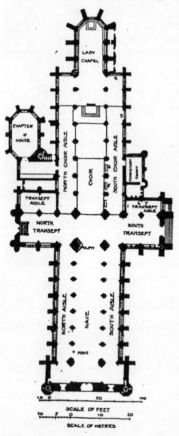

rising in graceful precision above the smooth expanse of an old mill-pool on the south side. It is built of an attractive reddish sandstone, but at close range the effect is disappointing, for the fabric has suffered so drastically at the hands of destroyers and restorers that its present appearance is rather that of an elaborate production of the nineteenth century. The west front is the dominant feature of the composition (61), and at a fair distance at least its appearance can have changed little since its completion early in the fourteenth century. With the exception of the turrets at the north and south corners, it is a flat façade designed purely for surface treatment, consisting of two spire-capped towers with a steep gable between. The elaborate scheme of decoration, largely destroyed in the seven-teenth and eighteenth centuries, was in three stages, consisting of close-set ranges of canopied statues which have been almost entirely replaced by Victorian banalities. The great west door is largely a reconstruction, with modern statues, of a strikingly beautiful and original design, and the north and south portals are of rather similar type, with double lancet apertures within large containing arches of many orders of carved moldings, that on the north being of the two the more elaborate. These also, however, have been to a great extent rebuilt, with modern statues. The central tower is surmounted by the largest of

61 LICHFIELD : The West Front, with its Spires and surface decoration
of sculpture, now almost entirely renewed

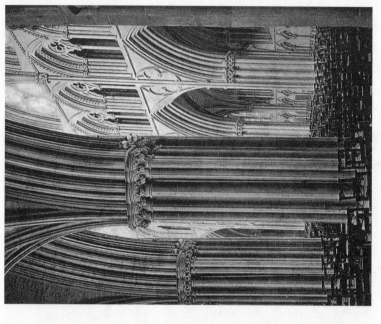

62 LICHFIELD : The Interior of the Chapter-house

63 LICHFIELD : A Glimpse of the Nave from the
North Aisle

the three spires, traditionally reconstructed by Sir Christopher Wren to replace the original work destroyed in the Civil War.

The building of the first Saxon church at Lichfield is attributed to Bishop Hedda at the close of the seventh century, for which it is probable that Roman ruins in the neighbourhood served as quarries. Nothing is known of the history of this church, or of the others that possibly succeeded it, but it is certain from recent excavations that a new cathedral was begun on a much larger scale under the first Norman bishop, Robert de Lymesey, towards the close of the eleventh century. The destruction during the Civil War of most of the archives and documents relating to the fabric left its earlier history rather nebulous, but there is little doubt that work on the present structure began with the building of the three western bays of the quire at the close of the twelfth century, ultimately remodelled with the later work. The evolution of the cathedral in its present form occupied a period of roughly a century and a quarter, culminating in the building of the Lady Chapel during the splendid episcopate of Walter Langton (1296–1321), a friend of Edward I and Lord Treasurer of England, who at the same time erected a shrine to St. Chad at the then enormous cost of £2,000. Langton was also responsible for the fortification of the close, which he surrounded with an embattled wall that remained standing until the Civil War, when in 1643 the precincts were occupied by the Royalists against a besieging force led by the fanatical Lord Brooke, who was "so great a zealot against the established discipline of the Church, that no less than the utter extirpation of Episcopacy, and abolishing all decent order in the service of God, would satisfy him; to which end he became leader of all the power he could raise for the destruction of the cathedral of Coventry and Litchfield." Brooke, while planting his canon against the south-east gate of the close, was shot dead by a sniper from the parapet of the main steeple; but despite what was taken by many for a direct portent of the divine will, the close was for three days subjected to a gruelling bombardment which wrought terrible havoc on the building, followed after its surrender by a wholesale desecration of the interior by Roundhead soldiery. It was recorded that at the Restoration the vestry was the only part left with a roof where it was pessible to conduct service, and it is to the credit of the first bishop of the new *régime*, the admirable Hackett, that he devoted immense energy and vast sums to the restoration of the battered cathedral to something approaching its ancient dignity.

Spick-and-span from the hands of its refurbishers, Professor Prior has described the interior in its final state in stern language, as "offensive to taste, for the same reason that china reproductions of the Venus of Milo or the oleographs of the Sistine Madonna are offensive." The plates of Britton's monograph of 1820 show a work of considerable decorative magnificence sadly damaged and decayed, but the restorers, much as their work was essential and admirable as were their intentions, are to be blamed for electing to reconstruct rather than repair, causing an inevitable falsification that is all too apparent. The nave is a rich design of circa 1250–1280, consisting of a closely spaced arcade of bold multiple moldings, with well-carved capitals and graceful cinquefoils in the spandrels, surmounted by a tall arcaded triforium of some elaboration, and a clerestory of curved triangular windows (63). The great arches at the crossing are particularly fine, carried on lofty clustered piers, and the transepts are of slightly earlier date than the nave, ending in the north in a group of five tall lancets, and in the south in a large Perpendicular window. Of the quire, the three western bays, as has been seen, were early Transitional work of the close of the twelfth century, but with the addition of the remaining four bays a little over a century later, the whole was remodelled, and the present clerestory added. The resulting design dispenses with a triforium, but in the lower portion of each tall clerestory window is a section of cusped panelling, with a miniature battlemented parapet to each bay, which takes its place. The entire range of windows is lined with a patterned relief of quatrefoils on the inner faces. The screen, reredos, and most of the fittings were introduced by Scott, who was also responsible for the listless statuary over the vaulting corbels. The beautiful sedilia are made up of fragments of the old reredos.

The Lady Chapel that forms an apsed termination to the east end is easily the finest part of the interior, with its steep-pitched vault and ranges of tall narrow windows patterned with trefoils in their heads—seven of them filled with exquisite old glass from the Cistercian abbey of Herkenrode in Belgium. The polygonal chapter-house (62), entered through a charming vestibule, adjoins the north transept, with which it is practically contemporary. It is vaulted from a central pier with a richly foliated capital, and lined continuously with wall-arcading. Its upper storey is used as a library, and contains some rare medieval manuscripts.

FROM THE MILL-POOL TO THE EAST

LINCOLN

The Cathedral Church of St. Mary

The abrupt hill commanding the Fens on which Lincoln Minster stands has been the site of a settlement since prehistoric times. On it the Romans built a city within massive quadrangular walls, fragments of which survive, and it is some gauge of its importance that it marked the point of intersection of no less than five imperial roads, including the Foss Way and Ermine Street. As a Saxon town it was converted to Christianity by Paulinus, the indomitable missionary bishop of York, in about 628, and a stone church was built on the site of the present St. Paul's in Bailgate. The original seat of the diocese, however, was the little village of Stow, about eleven miles north-west of the city, which has been identified as the ancient Sidnacester; and the church built there was created a bishopstool of the new diocese of Lindsey, maintaining its own line of bishops for over two hundred years. In about 870 the church at Stow was burnt by the Norsemen, and Lincoln itself fell into the hands of the invaders, and became the chief of the 'Five Boroughs' of the Danish Confederation. During the tenth century, the seat of the bishopric was removed for safety to Dorchester-on-Thames, in a remote corner of the diocese, and here it remained until after the Norman Conquest, when William's new bishop, Remigius of Fécamp, transferred it finally to Lincoln, where the building of a new castle and cathedral was almost immediately embarked upon. The Saxon inhabitants were forced to leave the hill and found their own settlement on the plain below, where the towers of their two churches still stand.

Remigius' church was some twenty years in building—a grim fortress-like structure, according to contemporary descriptions, part of the fabric of which is incorporated in the present west front. About 1141, the burning of the roof provided a pretext for the third bishop of the new line, Alexander the Magnificent, an ambitious and energetic builder, virtually to reconstruct the cathedral, and the rich Norman west doorways date from this period. During the reign of Stephen, the building was seized by the king and actually for some time garrisoned as a fortress; and its fabric must have suffered considerable damage through those stormy years, when Lincoln Castle, continually attacked and besieged, formed one of the most formidable strongholds of Matilda's faction. In 1185, however, on the 15th of April, some kind of earthquake or land subsidence occurred at Lincoln, severe enough to be felt almost throughout England, in which the Minster was "cleft from top to bottom." The damage done seems to have been beyond repair; but the next year a new bishop was appointed to the diocese, the

L

famous Hugh of Lincoln, under whose direction the building of a magnificent new cathedral, on revolutionary lines, was begun in 1192. "What Diocletian did at Spalato for the round arch," wrote Freeman, "St. Hugh did at Lincoln for the pointed arch." The great bishop did not live beyond 1200; but the work he had begun was slowly brought to maturity through the thirteenth century, largely under the supervision of another famous builder, Bishop Grosse-teste, culminating about 1280 in the completion of the presbytery, or 'Angel Choir,' "one of the loveliest of human works," designed as a seemly resting-place for the relics of the canonised founder. Its splendid consecration was attended by most of the crowned heads of Europe.

Lincoln to-day has still more of magnificence than any other English cathedral, a magnificence that begins with its situation. Its towered mass occupies the entire crown of its hill, and soars easily above the roofs of the old streets that twist and climb about it—in their turn placed high above the smoke and noise of the modern town. From the level fen country that spreads eastward, the profile of the great cathedral, reared on its hill, is a striking and conspicuous landmark for many miles.

With the exception of the three towers and the Norman nucleus of the west front, the Minster forms a splendidly complete epitome of the course of thirteenth-century building in England. Of its many façades, the most ambitious and striking is the great screen wall of the west front (64, 65), in which serried ranks of lancet arcading, extending some 171 feet from north to south, are broken by three tremendous shadowed cavities rising over the Norman doors. The section of unrelieved wall in which these are set formed part of the fabric of the original church, and its panels of Romanesque figure-carving contrast curiously with the uncomfortably seated figures of fourteenth-century kings ranged over the central door (65). It is impossible here to analyse in any detail the complex evolution of this remarkable composition; but whatever its merits or demerits as a unit, it is entirely unrelated to the design of the cathedral as a whole, and remains, as was intended, purely a screen, above which the twin Perpendicular towers, with their lower ranges of Romanesque arcading, rise a trifle abruptly.

With its double transepts and clustering chapels and porches, the cathedral spreads its masonry over a vast irregular plan, in a design that grows steadily in elaboration as it continues eastward. The eastern limb itself forms perhaps the richest building expression of its period in England (1216–1280), with its web of delicate Geo-metrical tracery and dignified ranges of panelled buttresses, termi-nat-ing in tall crocketed pinnacles and gablets. An unusual feature is the north and south doors to the presbytery, the latter, designed as a processional entrance for the consecration service, with a magnifi-cent sculptured porch now flanked by little Perpendicular chapels on either hand. On the north side is the chapter-house, with its enor-

64 LINCOLN : The Cathedral from the South-West, raised high on its hill above the city roofs

65   LICHFIELD : The Norman Core of West Front, with its tall shadowed
arches and sections of a Romanesque Sculptured Frieze

66 LINCOLN : The Main Vista through the Cathedral from West to East. The
Photograph gives an excellent impression of the scale and spaciousness of this
thirteenth-century giant

68   LINCOLN : The North Transept, with its fine Rose
Window called the 'Dean's Eye'

67   LINCOLN : The Chapter-house, the Prototype of
the characteristic English Polygonal Design, vaulted from
a Central Pier

mous radiating buttresses, adjoined by the green cloister garth, from
which is obtained one of the most remarkable views of the cathedral

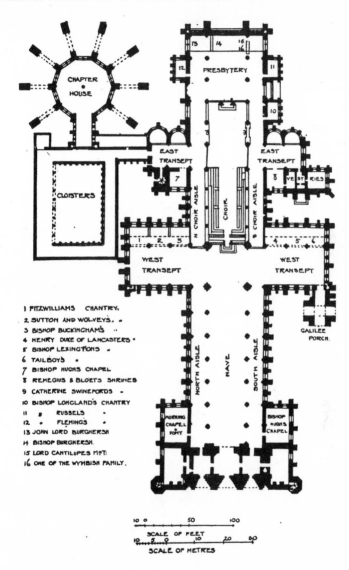

structure, rising in tier upon tier of fretted masonry, bristling with
pinnacles and spanned by graceful buttresses, the whole culminating
in one of the tallest and stateliest central towers in England, a

masterpiece of the early years of the fourteenth century, exquisite in proportion as in texture.

Entering by a west door, the first impression of the interior is one of spaciousness and restrained dignity, with a deftness and economy in execution which, compared with the heavier Anglo-Norman methods of some fifty years earlier, indicate a real revolution in building technique. If the nave (1209–1235) has one cardinal defect, it is a defect that characterises the major body of English work during the thirteenth century, namely the lowness of the vault; and this is accentuated at Lincoln by the particularly wide spacing of the main bays. Nevertheless, the design remains a splendidly youthful and vigorous achievement in early-Gothic building; and it is an experience not easily forgotten to stand at the west end and watch the swift retreat of the vault perspective towards the distant glint of the east window (66). Another memorable experience is to stand at the crossing, beneath the lightly poised 130-foot vault of the central tower, and enjoy the vistas down the main transepts (circa 1220), terminating northward in the great rose window called the 'Dean's Eye' (68), with its fine contemporary glazing, and southward in the leaf-like delicacy of the curvilinear 'Bishop's Eye,' filled with kaleidoscopic fragments of old glass. Both transepts have eastern aisles, each divided into three small chapels, and the stone screen at the crossing is a rich work of the early fourteenth century, flanked on either hand by elaborate thirteenth-century aisle doors, each with a magnificent display of sculpture in its arch-molds and capitals.

St. Hugh's own quire (1186–1200) was the first limb to be completed in the new cathedral. It consists of four aisled bays, terminating in narrow eastern transepts, each with a pair of small eastern chapels, and the work throughout is marked by impressive simplicity, almost amounting to severity, in the general design as in the detail. The vaulting constitutes a unique and rather worrying experiment in unsymmetrical ribbing, and a curious constructional device is the employment of two superimposed ranges of Purbeck arcading to strengthen the aisle walls. The seriousness and adolescent beauty of the structural effect contrasts' with the magnificent elaboration of the late fourteenth-century stallwork, which to-day forms the chief glory of St. Hugh's quire. Its forest of carved canopies is only comparable in richness with the slightly later work at Chester, and here also are splendid series of *poupée*-heads and misericords, the latter of a deftness and playfulness as charming as anything in English carving.

The lovely 'Angel Choir,' or presbytery (1256–1280), forms the culmination of the work at Lincoln, as it forms the culmination of the English style of the thirteenth century (6). It consists of five bays, terminating in a splendid Geometrical east window; and while its design manifestly owes much to earlier experiments, notably in the presbytery at Ely, the Lincoln work is so exquisite in proportion and detail, so rich without a hint of ostentation, that it thoroughly deserves the encomiums lavished upon it by many generations of ecclesiologists. Its chief effect is drawn from the intricate beauty of the narrow centre band of the triforium, a work of exquisite refinement in its crisp incisiveness of tracery and cusping. The arches spring from clustered Purbeck shafts, with richly carved capitals, and in the spandrels are the lovely angel figures that give the building its name. The slender vaulting shafts rest on foliated corbels in the spandrels of the great arcade, flanked on either side by trefoils, and the vault is of the usual low Lincoln springing, and weighs somewhat heavily on the fine Geometrical clerestory, with its remarkable interior duplication of tracery. The Angel Choir was designed to house the feretory of the bishop-founder, St. Hugh, one of the most important English shrines of the Middle Ages. This has of course vanished; but in the first northern bay stands the fourteenth-century Easter Sepulchre, with its profuse canopy-work and panelled reliefs of sleeping Roman soldiers; and at the east end, filling either side of the last bay, are some fine but badly broken tombs, including those of the Burghersh family. The east windows of the aisles retain their beautiful con-temporary glass.

The large decagonal chapter-house (67) is one of the earliest of its type in England, dating from the opening years of the thirteenth century. Its vaulted roof, however, supported by the characteristic central pier, is somewhat later than the rest of the building, though it is interesting to note that a similar expedient was employed at an early date at Lincoln (*circa* 1240) in the vaulting of the northern of the twin chapels that adjoin the western towers. The cloisters date from the close of the thirteenth century, and were built contrary to usage on the north side of the church and standing clear. Their north walk is occupied by the arcade of the beautiful library designed by Sir Christopher Wren, only preserved by a narrow margin during the last century from the destructive revivalism of the late J. L. Pearson, R.A.

THE EXPULSION FROM EDEN.
SPANDREL CARVING IN THE ANGEL CHOIR.'

M

LONDON

The Great Fire of 1666 hastened a process of gradual degenera-
tion that for over a hundred years had affected the fabric of Old
St. Paul's. Public affection for the great building, not unmixed with
civic parsimony, was expressed in belated attempts at patching
and reconditioning, and it was not until 1674, following an alarm-
ing minor collapse, that the Royal Commission appointed to enquire
into the matter finally decided on the demolition advocated by the
Surveyor-General of the King's Works, Sir Christopher Wren, who
had recently succeeded in this post the old poet-architect, Sir
John Denham. Born of cultured and comfortable stock, with
powerful Church connections, Wren's talents had won him early
recognition in the spheres of mathematics and astronomy. While
his qualifying experience in architecture can have been only slight
and theoretical, his approach to its practice was in the same spirit
of intense scientific enquiry that had already gained him supremacy
in other fields. The destruction by fire of much of medieval London
presented him with a stupendous opportunity, to which he rose
with characteristic vision and vigour; and though he was not
destined to rebuild it according to his great plan, provided while the
city still smoked, his talent was allowed free play in the reconstruction of its parish-churches, whose pale steeples, in a variety of
slender forms, rose one after another about the developing bulk of
the great cathedral, that was to provide the supreme reflection of
the spirit and churchmanship of the times.

The evolution of the design of St. Paul's is a subject of some
complexity, which necessarily can only be touched upon very
briefly. Already, before the Fire, Wren had put forward a scheme
for reconditioning the old fabric, previously on the outside clothed
in a classical coat by Inigo Jones, by remodelling the interior "after
a good Roman manner," and substituting for the tower at the
crossing a lofty "rotundo" surmounted by a stone lantern. When
the decision to rebuild was at last taken, the design he submitted
was of an originality far in advance of the times. Of a single storey
throughout, with a giant order, the plan to all intents and purposes
took the form of a Greek cross (later modified by the addition of a
short nave), with curving diagonal walls between the arms, and a
vast open space beneath the dome. Its rejection, which must have
been a bitter grief to Wren, was due chiefly to the ingrained conservatism of the clergy and the Catholic sympathies of the Court
party, neither of whom could tolerate the idea of a central preach
-ing space dominating the interior arrangement. Characteristically,

69   ST PAUL'S CATHEDRAL : A Western View from the Steeple of
St Martin's Ludgate

71 ST PAUL'S : The Cathedral from the South-West

70 ST PAUL'S : The South Quire Aisle and Stalls-Screen

73 ST PAUL'S : A View of the Nave from beneath
the Central Dome

72 ST PAUL'S : The Interior of the Quire, showing the
Stalls, Bishop's Throne, and Tijou's Ironwork Screen

74   ST PAUL'S CATHEDRAL :   Beneath Wren's great Central Dome, with a
glimpse of the Quire, and the beautiful carved Organ-Case

Wren's second design differed in almost every essential from the
first, reverting to the original cruciform plan, but preserving the

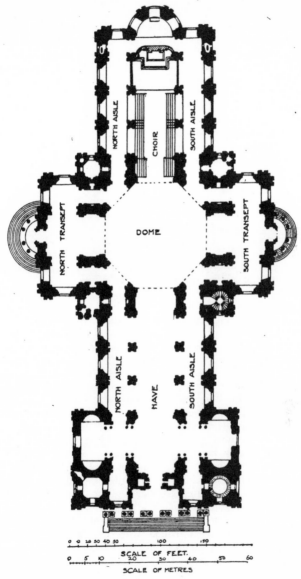

cherished idea of a central tholus and cupola, now surmounted by
a tall, rather curious spire. This design was approved by Royal

Warrant, but in the long course of execution suffered a process of modification at the hands of the architect that remains as mysterious as it is intriguing. Though adhering to the principles of the 'Warrant' plan, the character of the building underwent a radical transformation throughout, though the two-storeyed arrangement was maintained, principally because Wren was unable to obtain Portland stone in sufficient block for the giant order he favoured. The second storey is the screen-wall that has so troubled the purists, actually a legitimate and successful expedient for gaining height, and also serving a structural purpose in providing continuous abutment for the corner bastions of the great coffered arches supporting the dome.

The stone vaulting of the Warrant Design was replaced by a system of roofing with shallow saucer domes which constituted an absolute novelty. Wren's predilection for domical forms is a pronounced feature of his mature style—a style which, though certainly to some extent influenced by the academic vernacular of the Grande Régne, which he had studied on the spot in France, and by the engraved designs of Holland and baroque Italy, was chiefly informed by an instinct for what was seemly and appropriate to the English environment, with a fine breadth and fecundity in execution, and an unerring gift for proportion. All these qualities find expression in the St. Paul's dome—on the inside a vast airy lantern over the central space, on the outside a conspicuous and dignified landmark dominating the eighteenth-century city. The result is achieved con-structionally with great originality, by building a separate inner dome for interior effect, rising above which is a concealed brickwork cone that forms the core of the outer dome of leaded timber, and at the same time carries the crowning feature of the stone lantern, itself 70 feet high and of the stature of a parish steeple. This vast yet delicate mass, weighing 700 tons, poised above the circular sweep of the columnar peristyle, 'composes' magnificently with the intricate beauty of the western *campanili*, which, for all their memories of Borromini's Sant'Agnese, remain a creation of extraordinary skill and power.

A wealth of craftsmanship was employed on the building, which it was Wren's peculiar genius that he could so control and co-ordinate that it might have been the work of a single hand. The standard of execution was superb throughout; and while the extent to which the architect provided designs of ornamental features remains uncertain, there can be little doubt that a bond of sympathetic understanding existed between Wren and his craftsmen which allowed the latter to a great extent to interpret his requirements, even when not provided with drawings "in the great." The masonry was preponderantly of Portland stone, though a variety of other materials were used for special purposes; and Joshua Marshall and Thomas Strong were the first master-masons, the latter afterwards succeeded by his son, Edward. A huge quantity of material from the old cathedral was used for the filling of the ashlar-faced walls, and here the inexperience of the age in construction on a cathedral scale must be blamed for the building up of the main dome supports in this fashion, necessitating in our own time a vast programme of strengthening only recently completed. A large body of carvers was employed to execute the ornamental stonework, and since the pay was good (from the special tax on coal imposed for the fabric-fund), the best talent was attracted. In addition to those mentioned, the outstanding names are Nathaniel Rawlins, Ephraim Beauchamp, the Kempsters, Christopher and William (the latter mainly responsible for the south-west tower), and, better known as woodcarvers, Jonathan Maine and Grinling Gibbons, the greatest of them all, the broad elegance of whose style impressed itself upon the entire decorative work of the cathedral. In addition to the rich stone swags under the quire windows (at £13 apiece), Gibbons, with his trained staff, executed the beautiful wreaths in the spandrels of the quarter-domes (at £32 apiece), and many of the delightful cherub forms that are a favourite ornamental feature. The chief statuaries were Caius Gabriel Cibber, the Holsteiner, and Francis Bird, who, among other works, carved the great relief of the Conversion of St. Paul in the west pediment for £650.

The head carpenter was Richard Jennings, later succeeded by John Longland, who supervised the building of the roofs and domes, and Charles Hopson was the most important of a group of joiners. The splendid furniture of the quire, including the stalls and organ-cases, was carved by Grinling Gibbons and his assistants, while Jonathan Maine carried out the woodwork in the library and the screens of the western chapels. The superb ironwork was almost entirely created by the Huguenot, Jean Tijou, at his workshop at Hampton Court, who may be said to have established an English revival in this craft. The screens, gates and grilles of the quire, with their rich varied designs and masterly treatment of acanthus leafage, were his supreme achievement, together with the elaborate overthrow of the Geometrical staircase in the south-west tower. The great dome was decorated on the inside by Sir James Thornhill (whose work until recently was covered with a six-inch beard of dirt), rather against the wishes of Wren, who would have preferred a lining of mosaic "as is nobly executed in the Cupola of St. Peter's in Rome." Marble painting was much employed at the east end, not as a subterfuge but as a delicate art of the time, for the rare marbles intended were ruled out on the score of expense. Over the altar was to have been a marble *baldachino*, but this was never executed; the present reredos, so ostentatiously uncomfortable in both scale and design, is a comparatively recent addition. The appropriateness of the modern mosaics by Salviati and Sir William Richmond can also be criticised. The monuments, however, form in general an impressive series, thoroughly consistent with the serene classicism of their surroundings; and among these mention must be made of the splendid Wellington tomb, which is the work of Alfred Stevens.

N

NORWICH

THE CATHEDRAL CHURCH OF THE HOLY TRINITY

The year 630 marked the final conversion to Christianity of East Anglia, when the Burgundian monk Felix, its first bishop, established his see at the Suffolk port of Dunwich, now utterly vanished as a result of coast erosion. In 660 the great diocese was subdivided by Archbishop Theodore, and both Dunwich and Elmham in Suffolk were the seats of bishops until about 950, when it was once again united at the latter. In 1075 the bishopric was removed to Thetford, but in 1094 it was finally established at Norwich in compliance with the decree of Lanfranc's Synod that all sees should be ·fixed in the principal town of their diocese. Herbert de Losinga was the first Bishop of Norwich, a Norman-Benedictine careerist owing his early advancement to simony that was flagrant even for his period. But on the assumption of his bishop's office he seems genuinely, if somewhat belatedly, to have repented of his disreputable association with Rufus; "I entered on mine office disgracefully," he wrote in a letter that has been preserved, "but by the help of God's grace I shall pass out of it with credit." The founding of a cathedral and great religious house at Norwich, on a scale commensurate with the dignity of his famous Order, was considered to have been undertaken as a partial expiation of former irregularities.

The foundation stone of Norwich Cathedral was laid in 1096, and the building of the Norman fabric seems to have occupied some forty years. In about 1170, however, a fire broke out in the monastic quarters, which spread to the church, and probably partially destroyed the Lady Chapel, which formed the central feature of the apsidal *chevet*. This event, combined with the growing cult of Our Lady during the thirteenth century, determined Bishop Suffield to demolish what remained of the chapel and rebuild it about 1250 on a more lavish scale in the current Gothic manner. His work, however, falling into disrepair after the Reformation, was destroyed under Dean Gardiner towards the close of the sixteenth century. In 1271 rioting broke out in the city against the monks, whose unpopularity had reached a climax under the fierce and truculent despotism of Prior William de Brunham. Something like a pitched battle took place in Tombland, lasting for several days, in which many lives were lost and the cathedral gutted by fire to its stone walls. Sentence of excommunication was passed on the city, Henry III himself travelled to Norwich to preside at the trial of the leaders, and vast sums were extorted from the townsmen to repair the damage. The final misfortune occurred in 1361, when the wooden spire and part of the central tower collapsed in a gale, severely injuring the eastern limb. This resulted in the

75 NORWICH : The Cathedral from the South-East, showing the tall Perpendicular Clerestory of the Quire and Norman South Transept

76 NORWICH : The Norman Nave, with its Fifteenth-Century Lierne Vault,
studded with Sculptured Bosses

building of the fourteenth-century clerestory to the quire; and the main body of the church was finally fireproofed by the construction of a stone lierne vault under Bishop Lyhart about 1446.

Despite these additions, Norwich to-day, more than any other English cathedral with the exception of Durham, retains the appearance and characteristics of a great Anglo-Norman abbey church. The west front, never very striking in design, was reduced to insignificance by Blore in 1875, but the long north and south elevations of the nave rise like cliffs, scarred by intricate strata-bands of arches, arcades and windows. The transepts were rebuilt with plain Norman fronts, and the southern is another example of how literal refacing can rob a façade of its charm and character. The eastern limb is easily the most beautiful part of the building (75), the tall lantern-like clerestory of the Perpendicular reconstruction, with its delicate precision of window tracery and lofty ring of flying buttresses, rising high above the close-knit Romanesque texture of the original presbytery, with its *chevet* of apsidal chapels, rare in England. The recent addition that takes the place of the Lady Chapel is a memorial to the fallen of the last war. The Norman tower at the crossing is very rich and magnificent, with its horizontal bands of Romanesque pattern-ing, flanked by buttresses of vertical shafting that rise to crocketed pin-nacles at the four corners. It is surmounted by a tall spire that forms a dignified landmark over the flatter surrounding country, and is perhaps best seen from Old Crome's Mousehold Heath, or from over the Wensum by the water-gate to the precincts at Pull's Ferry.

CARVED BOSS, "THE LAST SUPPER" IN THE NAVE VAULT

Probably the first impression on entering the cathedral is of the exceptional length of the Norman nave, extending through fourteen bays, and of its great height (76). The yellowish stone appears warm and mellow in the full even lighting of the interior, and the general effect is one of homogeneous texture and solid dignity. A remarkable feature of the design, probably dictated by require-ments of lighting, is the height of the single-arch triforium, which equals that of the main arcade; and despite its general uniformity, the nave can show occasional vagaries, such as the massive cylindri-cal diapered piers of the ninth bay from the east, marking the original western termination of the cathedral, and the two bays of elegant sixteenth-century reconstruction introduced by Bishop Nix for his personal chantry. The aisles are roofed with a simple Norman groined vault, in contrast with the elaboration of the lierne work of the nave roof (76), which ranks among the finest achievements of English medieval masoncraft. As has been seen, it was built during the later fifteenth century in the episcopate of Walter Lyhart, whose rebus of a stag lying in water appears on every other vaulting shaft; and a striking feature is its profusion

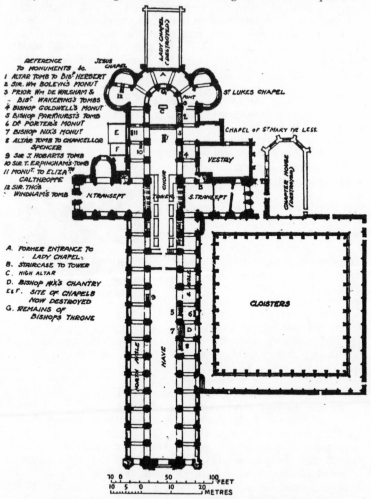

of sculptured bosses, which extend in three ranges from east to west, comprising in the nave alone some 328 subjects, illustrating in graphic and homely idiom the course of Bible history from the Creation to the Apocalypse. These bosses have recently been cleaned and touched with bright colour to give an approximation of their original effect.

At the crossing, the tower repeats on the interior something of the rich patterning of its exterior faces, though the swagged Renaissance ceiling that appears in Britton's engravings did not survive the nineteenth century. The organ screen is a modern adaptation, but between the transepts and the quire aisles, the Romanesque arches have been filled with beautiful screens of open Perpendicular tracery, erected under Prior Catton about 1509. The eastern limb is short in comparison with the nave, but architecturally

THE PRIOR'S DOOR IN THE CLOISTER

is without question the finest part of the cathedral (77). The Norman design extends through arcade and triforium, and above it rises the lofty lightly poised canopy of Bishop Percy's clerestory, with its great areas of glazing admitting a flood of light into the quire. It is remarkable how this fifteenth-century transformation blends with the massive Romanesque of three centuries earlier, and the whole with the delicate lierne vaulting that spreads its web over the roof above. The view culminates eastward in the semicircular sweep of the apse, which, with its radiant lighting effects and soaring complexity of arch and vault, forms perhaps the most effective background in any English cathedral for the high altar (77).

The ambulatory around the apse forms a continuation of the

groined-vaulted presbytery aisles. From this open a number of small chapels and chantries, among the most interesting being the two remaining chapels of the apsidal *chevet*, which are so conspicuous a feature of the exterior design. Each is formed of two separate segments of a circle, and in the little Jesus Chapel, traces of the original painting have been used as a basis for the reconstruction of the medieval polychromatic scheme. The cloister garth is on the south side, between nave and transept, and the fourteenth-century Prior's Door that gives access from it to the cathedral is very elaborate and magnificent, with canopied figures of saints and bishops ranged in stellar radiations around the arch. The cloister itself is broad and spacious, and its tracery of several periods covers a wide range of curvilinear and Perpendicular pattern. It contains much of interest, such as the remains of the monks' *lavatorium* and bookshelves, and, as at Gloucester, the holes in the flagstones for the novices' games; but perhaps its finest feature is the series of sculptured bosses in the vaulting, which, though uncleaned and unrepaired, are almost the equal for variety and interest of those of the nave. The thirteenth-century chapter-house was pulled down by Dean Gardiner at the same time as the Lady Chapel, but the Choir School of the twelfth and thirteenth centuries, with its ribbed stone vault, remains and is worth a visit. The close contains some beautiful and interesting old houses, and is entered from Tombland by two splendid gateways in the local flint flushwork—the Ethelbert Gate, erected as part of the penance of the townsfolk after the riot of 1271, and the Erpingham Gate, built as a memorial to Sir Thomas Erpingham, Shakespeare's "white-headed knight" of Agincourt, designed by the famous Norfolk mason, William Hindley, later master of the work for the York quire, who modelled it on the great centre arch of the Peterborough west front.

FROM THE SOUTH-WEST

77 NORWICH : The Quire and Apse, showing the tall windows of the
later Clerestory, and elaborate Lierne Vault

78 OXFORD : The Quire looking East, showing the remarkable Fifteenth-
Century Vault. The East End is a reconstruction by Scott

OXFORD

The Cathedral Church of Christ (formerly St. Frideswide's)

Though accounts of the early virginal struggles of St. Frideswide are largely romantic legend, it is at least historical that she lived and founded a priory at Oxford, which, after various vicissitudes, settled down in 1122 as an Augustinian house, with one Guimond as first prior. If the conscientious researches of the late J. Park Harrison may be accepted, the three rough arches in the lower part of the east wall are part of the original church, dating from as early as 727; and the foundations of three small eastern apses have also been discovered. Though the records on the point make confused reading, it seems that this church was ultimately burnt over the heads of a party of marauding Danes in *circa* 1100; and after considerable enlargement and reconstruction, the relics of St. Frideswide were translated to the present building in 1180. The Lady Chapel was added during the thirteenth century, the so-called Latin (properly St. Christopher's) Chapel followed about a century later, and the famous quire

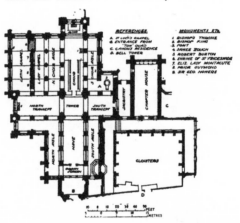

vault dates from *circa* 1480. Early in the sixteenth century, the great Wolsey tore down the three western bays of the nave to build 'Tom Quad', and, but for his disgrace in 1529, the rest of St. Frideswide's would have followed to make way for the new chapel of Cardinal College, which would probably have surpassed in magnificence even that of King's at Cambridge.

The building as it stands can be described as the smallest, shyest and squarest of the English cathedrals, incorporating in its fabric some of the oldest masonry in the country. Hemmed in by private gardens and the later ranges of Christchurch, of which it now forms the college chapel, its situation is unobtrusive to say the least of it; from the green expanse of Tom Quad, all that can be seen is the rather squat low thirteenth-century spire rising above the east walk, and the approach is by small and insignificant archways, one of them giving access to a miniature Perpendicular cloister. Truncated westward, the addition of the two lateral chapels on the north side results in an almost square plan, and the internal effect is unusual and confusing. Of the main Norman design of the interior, the most remarkable feature is the arrangement of the arcade, in which an illusion of greater height is obtained by building up the heavy cylindrical piers, with their interesting early carved capitals, and throwing over the small blind triforium massive round arches that rise as high as the clerestory cill (78). As a result, the arches of the true arcade spring from half-way down the piers, carried on small intermediate capitals that also receive the aisle-vaulting. The same device for gaining apparent height was used in the quire of Jedburgh Abbey and in two bays of the nave at Romsey.

The nave is ceiled with a fine open-timber roof, panelled in small compartments; but the glory of the building is the beautiful and individual design of the quire vault (78), a work of rare interest as showing the structural transition to fan-vaulting, of a type which in Oxford had been employed with notable success a few years earlier in the splendid roof of the Divinity School. In the latter, the great four-centred sustaining arches span the building in full view; at St. Frideswide's they disappear behind the conoids, while at Henry VII's chapel at Westminster they are entirely invisible. The central area of the vault is patterned with cusped lierne ribs, which in each compartment unite in a rich and elaborate openwork pendant. The east end of the quire was reconstructed by Scott with a rather clumsy wheel window, and the sober Jacobean fittings shown in Britton's views were replaced at this time.[1] The plain thirteenth-century Lady Chapel is adjoined laterally by the beautiful curvilinear Latin Chapel, and the vistas from one to the other are complex and unusual. The latter contains some fine old glass, with a complete range of fifteenth-century stalls and a Jacobean reading desk and pulpit. There are some notable monuments and effigies, and the watching-loft of St. Frideswide's shrine incorporates magnificent Perpendicular screenwork in wood and stone, though the carved base of the tomb itself only represents a piecing together of smashed fragments. It is cause for satisfaction that even one of Van Linge's fine seventeenth-century Flemish windows has survived an outbreak of tasteless Victorian glazing, though a word must be said for the work of Burne-Jones in several windows, which is of a restful delicacy and pallor. The rectangular chapter-house, entered through a Norman door in the cloister, is a pleasing interior of simple thirteenth-century design.

[1] Some of this stallwork has found its way to Cassington Church, Oxfordshire, together with the brass candelabra.

79 PETERBOROUGH : The Great Arches of the West Front. The little
Porch in the centre is a fifteenth-century addition

80   PETERBOROUGH : The Norman Nave, with its Thirteenth-Century
Diapered Timber Ceiling

PETERBOROUGH

The earlier history of the Benedictine monastery of St. Peter forms a remarkable parallel to that of Ely. Situated on the edge of the Fens, it owed its foundation to the conversion to Christianity of Peada, King of the Mercians, in about 665. Medeshamstede (the homestead in the meadows) was the first name given to the settlement that formed around the abbey buildings, but, with the growth of the establishment through the Middle Ages, the more portentous 'Burgh of St. Peter' was adopted; and indeed, until the coming of the Great Northern Railway in the 'fifties of the last century' transformed the character of the place, it remained a remote and almost unique survival of the medieval monastic borough, quietly ruled by a Dean and Chapter, just as for centuries previous it had been ruled by its Abbot. As at Ely, the original establishment was sacked and gutted by the Danes in about 870, and rehabilitated some hundred years later under Edwin, when a new church was built, very magnificent for its period. With the Conquest, a Norman abbot was appointed to St. Peter's, which, like Ely, had its secular importance as an outpost for the supervision of the unconquered Fens; and during the last phase of his resistance, the Abbey was attacked by the Saxon patriot Hereward, with a mixed band of Danes and English, who destroyed all but the church where he himself had taken the vows of knighthood. Not many years later this too was damaged beyond repair in a great fire; and its reconstruction on a far larger scale and in its present form was undertaken almost immediately under Abbot John of Sais, the foundation stone being laid in 1118.

The building of the Norman Minster occupied a period of roughly eighty years, during which the work was continued by leisurely stages in accordance with the original design, notwithstanding the momentous changes in construction and ornament that accompanied the transition to Gothic. It is doubtful whether the new church was ever completed with a Norman west front, but it seems certain that the nave was extended westward towards the close of the twelfth century, while in the opening years of the thirteenth the present unique and magnificent screen-front (79) was added under either Abbot Andrew or Acharius, though there is not the smallest reference in the chronicles to its building. The work must have been completed by 1237, however, for in that year the Minster was finally consecrated by the famous Grosseteste, Bishop of Lincoln. Towards the close of the thirteenth century a sumptuous Lady Chapel was built that has not survived, and the last considerable addition was made at the close of the fifteenth century, when

O

71

the magnificent 'New Building,' or retro-quire, was erected under Abbots Ashton and Kirton. Soon after, in 1541, the reign of the abbots ended, and the Minster became a cathedral, possibly owing its preservation to the presence in the nave of the tomb of Katherine of Aragon, whom Henry VIII had promised should be remembered by "one of the goodliest monuments in Christendom." It seems to have fallen into considerable disrepair under the Stuarts, and with the Commonwealth was subjected by Cromwell's troops to one of the most callously destructive outbreaks of iconoclasm of the seventeenth century, in which monuments, chantries, furniture, and indeed every malleable fitting, were smashed or mutilated beyond repair, and even the fabric of the church shaken. Towards the end of the century it was necessary for the townsmen to demolish

THE CATHEDRAL FROM THE NORTH-WEST

the Lady Chapel and sell the materials for funds to effect urgent structural repairs; and despite the loss to architecture, it is to their credit that sufficient local affection remained for the great building to save it from otherwise inevitable decay.

To-day little remains of the secluded cathedral city, where sedan chairs were still to be seen about the precincts in the 'forties of the last century; and modern Peterborough has emerged as a considerable railway and manufacturing centre, of which the close forms a quiet backwater. In spite of the flatness of the surrounding country, the cathedral does not stand out boldly above the landscape as at Ely, but lies squat and low, though there are pleasant views of it from the flats to eastward, towards the ruined sister-foundations of Crowland and Thorney. At close range, the elevations of nave and transepts are unremarkable as façades, and tell a not unusual story of Norman arcading and fenestration adapted and enlarged

81 PETERBOROUGH : The Retro-Quire, or 'New Work' of the
Fifteenth Century, with its fine Fan Vault

82   RIPON : The Cathedral from the South-East

83   RIPON : The Quire looking East, with a glimpse of the Stalls

to the lighting requirements of later periods. The low central
tower was rebuilt by Pearson, and the short eastern limb retains the
original apse, with the addition of large blunt-headed curvilinear
windows. Here an unusual effect is produced by a semicircular
Norman upper stor-
ey rising above the
square-ended lower
stage of the fif-
teenth- century 'New
Build- ing,' that forms
the actual eastern
termi- nation of the
church. But easily the
most striking feature
of the exterior is the
west front, an aston-
ishing *tour de force* of
thir- teenth-century
de- sign, incorporating
three immense portals
that emulate and even
rival the sculptured
caverns of the Ile de
France (79). A possi-
ble criticism would be
the comparative slen-
derness of the flank-
ing towers, with their
graceful fourteenth-
century spires; and
of the two great
towers of the western
transepts that were to
rise behind the main
screen, only one was
completed, and that
has lost its wooden
spire. The rich gables
over the portals in-
corporate wheel win-
dows and preserve
their contemporary
sculpture, and the

THE SOUTH GABLE AND SPIRE OF THE WEST
FRONT

whole design is of an audacity and greatness of conception
certainly more effective than the rather heterogeneous compromise
of the Lincoln façade, and interesting to compare in treatment
with the rich west-country plasticity of the work at Wells. The
small fifteenth-century porch placed within the central arch hardly

seems to detract from the equilibrium of the design as a whole.

Entering the cathedral at the west, the long Romanesque nave

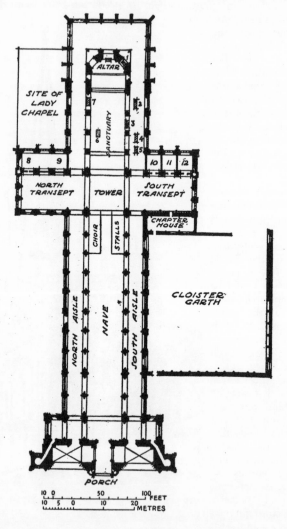

of eleven bays is dignified and well-proportioned, with a slightly more elaborate treatment of triforium and clerestory than at either Ely or Norwich (80). This design, which is continued with only minor variations in the piers throughout the cathedral, reveals once again the ingrained conservatism of twelfth-century Benedictine building. The main body of the work at Peterborough was not completed until 1193, and it is significant to compare its final phase with the design of St. Hugh's quire at Lincoln, which is practically its contemporary. The aisles, with their effective ranges of interlaced wall-arcading, are roofed with quadripartite vaults, but the nave itself was never vaulted in stone, and retains its original canted wooden ceiling—a work of extraordinary interest, preserving its contemporary painted diaper decoration. The western door into the cathedral is one of the earliest specimens of English church woodwork, ornamented with a giant lattice pattern incorporating an archaic carved capital in the centre.

In their severe simplicity, the transepts are one of the most effective features of the cathedral, each with eastern chapels that incorporate some pleasant fifteenth-century screenwork of local type. They are ceiled in wood, and terminate in trios of Perpendicular windows filling the original Norman apertures. The shortness of the quire is a disappointment, and like the nave and transepts it has a timber ceiling, which in the western bays makes some attempt to imitate a lierne vault. The apse itself, however, is flat-roofed, and lighted by a triple range of curvilinear windows, of which the upper retain their old glass, and the lower open unglazed upon the later retro-quire. The stalls are entirely modern, the tessellated marble pavement was laid down during the last century, and Pearson's preposterous *baldachino* over the high altar is as inappropriate as it is illegal in an English cathedral. The only early fittings that remain are the fifteenth-century brass eagle lectern, the magni-ficent panelled chest in the south transept, and the adorable little double-piscina in the south aisle, which has its counterpart in the south-western chapel.

Some of the finest work in the cathedral is in the fifteenth-century retro-quire (81) that envelops the apse in its lower storeys, to which brief reference has already been made. No original glass remains in its tall Perpendicular windows, but these admit a flood of light to the interior, giving full effect to the decorative elegance of the stone panelling, with its varied range of devices that include the Tudor rose and portcullis, cross-keys and croziers, and the rebuses and ciphers of the abbot builders. The whole is roofed by one of the finest fan vaults in England. In this, the central bosses between the fans are each of them over a ton in weight, and carved with a variety of similar devices, including St. Peter's keys. The chapter-house was destroyed after the Reformation, and of the cloisters, only the boundary wall and the stumps of the vaulting shafts remain, with traces of a *lavatorium* on the south side. The Norman Prior's Door into the cathedral in the north-east corner is exceptionally sumptuous. Two ranges of arches of the thirteenth-century infirmary are standing, a few built curiously into the fronts of later prebendal houses. The close contains some interesting old buildings and two fine gateways.

RIPON

The monastery of Ripon was founded in the seventh century by Celtic monks from Melrose and Iona, but following the ratification of the papal authority in England by the Synod of Whitby, it was bestowed upon the famous Romanist, St. Wilfrid, himself probably a native of the district. From his travels in the South,

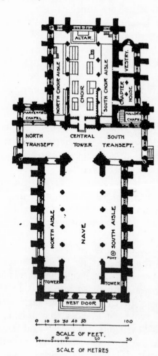

Wilfrid had absorbed something of the latent culture of Italy, and his enthusiasm for building found ex-pression in the basilicas of Hexham and Ripon, and in the adornment of St. Peter's at York. It seems possible that the present Saxon crypt of the cathedral is the work of his period. In 678, Ripon was raised to a bishopric for a few years, but, on the death of Bishop Eadhed, the church reverted once again to the Augustinians, and in the tenth century was re-established as a foundation for secular canons, which it remained throughout the Middle Ages, forming a supplementary bishopstool of the vast diocese of York. It was not until 1836 that it was once more promoted to cathedral rank.

It seems fairly certain that Ripon Minster was either rebuilt or remodelled by Thomas of Bayeux, the first Norman Archbishop of York, at the close of the eleventh century, though the Norman crypt and apse of the vestry are all that remain from this period. During the later twelfth century, however, it was entirely reconstructed by Archbishop Roger Pont l'Evêque, who had already inaugurated a considerable building programme at York; and the new design, of which Sir George Gilbert Scott was the first to point out the extraordinary interest, forms a unique expression of the transition at its most delicate juncture from Norman Romanesque to English early Gothic. As was then customary in collegiate churches, the nave was built broad and without aisles, with the lower storey of the walls left plain. A tall blind arcade of considerable complexity rose from the first string-course, divided by delicate vaulting shafts that are the direct precursors of the sleder Purbeck that later became a character-istic of the thirteenth century; and the clerestory predicts its graceful lancet forms. Archbishop Roger's design can now only be seen in the tran-septs, and in isolated bays of the nave and quire, but its archi-tectural importance is unmistakeable, for it provides a further insight into the aspira-tions of the Tran-sitional builders to-wards a national ex-pression in Gothic.

One of the smallest of the English cath-edrals, Ripon stands on rising ground in pleasantly pastoral surroundings (82). Today it loses some-what in general effect by the disappearance of the three lead spires that formerly rose from the central and western tow-ers; and towards the middle of the last century, Scott's 'puri-fi-cation' of the west front, including the removal of the tracery and mullions from the fourteenth-cen-tury windows, gave it a rather barren and

ARCHBISHOP ROGER'S DESIGN IN THE NORTH-WESTERN BAY OF THE NAVE

featureless air. The nave and western bays of the quire, with their fine ranges of large uniform windows, are of Perpendicular recon-struction, and the transepts of the Transitional design. The most distinctive part of the structure is the eastern bays of the quire, which, with its vast Geometrical east window and graceful flying buttresses, is finely typical of the final phase of early Gothic in Yorkshire, as it also expresses itself at Guisborough and a little later at Selby.

The interior, in which no less than six building periods are evident, is a remarkable patchwork even for an English cathedral. The nave is a pleasing Perpendicular reconstruction, but the main features of Archbishop Roger's design are preserved in the first two bays, now forming the inner faces of the western towers. The latter's work also remains untouched in the north transept, but the south was remodelled at a later period. After the collapse of two sides of the central tower in about 1450, it was necessary to rebuild the great arches at the crossing. This work was still uncompleted at the time of the Reformation, when it was abandoned, which explains the eccentric appearance of the western arch, with its lofty clustered Perpendicular casing on the south side only (84). The stone screen placed across it is a dignified work of the later fifteenth century.

The first two bays of the quire on the north side are Archbishop Roger's work, and face across to corresponding bays of Perpendicular reconstruction on the south. The three eastern bays are of a distinctive and homogeneous design of about 1290 (83), with a glazed triforium and inner duplication of tracery screening the clerestory windows, terminating eastward in a vast and magnificent Geometrical window of seven lights. The vault is a passable timber reconstruction by Scott, incorporating a series of the original carved bosses; but the chief interest of the Ripon quire lies in its stallwork, which ranks among the finest achievements of later fifteenth-century craftsmanship. The two tiers of canopies are delicately designed and intricately carved, and there is a vigorous series of misericords, very charming in their treatment of scriptural subjects. The ornate stone sedilia provide a touch of fourteenth-century exuberance.

The rectangular building between the quire and the south transept, apsed in its lower storey, is used as a chapter-house and vestry. As has been seen, it is the only portion of the cathedral, with the exception of the crypt beneath it, that incorporates Romanesque work, though this was largely remodelled in Archbishop Roger's time, and the circular windows inserted. The low, massively ribbed vault probably dates from a few years later. The building is of three storeys, with an upper chapel, or Lady Loft, added about 1330, now used as a library.

84 RIPON : The Great Arches of the Crossing; an Uncompleted Reconstruction.
The fine Stone Screen is of the Fourteenth Century

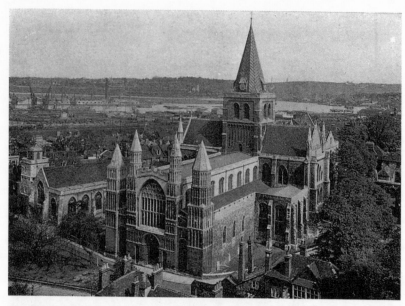

85 ROCHESTER : A Bird's-eye View of the Cathedral beside the Medway, with the adjoining Church of St Nicholas, built by the Monks to settle a dispute with the secular congregation

86 ROCHESTER : The Norman Arcade of the Nave

ROCHESTER

The bishoprics of Rochester and London are, with the single exception of Canterbury, the oldest in England, having been founded by St. Augustine in 601. Justus was the first Bishop of Rochester, one of the band sent from Rome by St. Gregory to help Augustine's mission, and the earliest church was dedicated to St. Andrew, the patron saint of his own monastery on the Caelian Hill. The pre-Conquest history of the cathedral was one of almost incessant war and danger, but with the establishment of the Normans, the scarred Saxon building was finally demolished in about 1080 by Bishop Gundulf, and a new church begun for a quire of some twenty Benedictine monks. About forty years later, this still uncompleted work was largely remodelled and recased under Bishops Ernulf (1115–1124) and John of Canterbury (1125–1137). The new church was dedicated in 1130, but successive fires ravaged the interior through the twelfth century, and in 1179 the monks began the enlargement and rebuilding of the eastern limb and transepts, which were completed about 1240, though work on the fabric continued intermittently through the next two hundred years. The Civil War saw a systematic spoliation of the fittings by Puritan soldiery, who "so far profaned this place as to make use of it in the quality of a tippling place, as well as dug several saw-pits, and the city joiners made frames for houses in it." The mischief done at this time, however, was negligible compared with that worked by Cottingham and Scott, whose successive restorations, covering much of the nineteenth century, repeat something of the history of Hereford.

To-day the cathedral lies unassumingly on the edge of its rather shabby old city, facing eastward across the Medway to the low line of the Kentish hills beyond (85). Modest in appearance and moderate in its dimensions, the nave and transepts represent a plain Norman fabric with some later fenestration, while the eastern limb shows a gradual and unassuming development from *circa* 1179 to 1240, somewhat falsified by its restorers. The broad, low and quite appropriate central tower, with its blunt spire, was built in 1904 as a substitute for Cottingham's weak creation; and the west front is an effective Norman composition of arcaded turrets and gables, rather reminiscent of the old design at Hereford, though instead of the curious central tower of the latter is a late embattled gable above a large Perpendicular window. On the north side of the quire stands the ruined shell of 'Gundulf's Tower,' surviving from the first Norman church, and here also the four-way gables of the thirteenth-century eastern transept turrets are an interesting and unusual feature. Generally speaking, however, the exterior can show little distinctive craftsmanship, though mention must be made of the fine sculptured Norman portal of the west front and the very elaborate fourteenth-century door of the chapter-room, with its saint statues and rich canopies.

The interior of the nave is a well-proportioned and impressive late-Norman design of massive compound piers of some diversity,

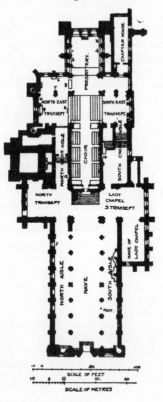

carrying a heavy arcade of chevron arches beneath a richly carved and diapered triforium (86). The clerestory windows are a Perpendicular insertion, and the two eastern bays were rebuilt to an undistinctive design of *circa* 1280. Despite the embryonic vaulting shafts, the nave was never roofed with stone, and the present workmanlike timber ceiling was probably added during the fifteenth century with the remodelling of the clerestory. The eastern limb is an unpretentious if rather fretful design, marred by a clumsy and excessive use of Purbeck marble in the attenuated vaulting shafts and shallow arcading of the unpierced quire walls; and what beauty and originality it possessed have been diminished by later restoration and bedizenment. Rochester is the only major English cathedral without a processional path around the high altar, and the well-lit presbytery occupies the usual position of the eastern chapel. The absence of the latter, however, is balanced by the addition of eastern transepts, each with an eastern aisle containing altars, and the quire is raised upon one of the finest crypts in the country, largely of thirteenth-century construction, with a heavy ribbed vault. There is an interesting series of bishops' tombs in good condition, finest among which is that of John de Sheppey, dating from *circa* 1360 and long concealed behind later masonry. Only scanty traces exist of the old conventual buildings, and the Norman chapter-house is a ruin.

ST. ALBANS

The church lies slightly apart from the town on a green slope, and the reddish tinges in its fabric, most apparent in the texture of the short tower (87), result from the use of old Roman tiles from the vanished city of Verulamium. Though the work in general is of an unambitious character, the building forms a remarkable patchwork in which almost every medieval style is represented. It was begun under Abbot Paul of Caen between 1077 and 1088 to replace the Benedictine church founded by Offa in 793; and there is the usual history of eastward extension during the thirteenth century, with the addition of a Lady Chapel in the current fashion. The nave, at 550 feet, is the second longest in Europe, and while its exterior design is generally unpretentious, the west front and transept faces, added by Lord Grimthorpe late in the last century, provide a deplorable instance of incongruous and opiniated revivalism. On the inside it incorporates three distinct designs (89), with first and foremost that of the Norman builders, heavy and rather archaic in character—almost an immensely solid wall with three stages of plain arched openings. The three western bays on the north and the four on the south side were added during the thirteenth century; and following a collapse, the fifth to the ninth bays from the west on the south side were also remodelled in *circa* 1345 to a somewhat similar design. This nave is ceiled throughout in plain oak, and there are interesting traces of the original painted scheme, including panels of the Crucifixion on the stone faces of six piers on the north side, presumably intended to back small altars (89).

The *pulpitum* is a stately work of *circa* 1360. Beyond it, the first three bays of the ritual quire continue the Norman design, and the transepts are remarkable for the occurrence of turned Saxon balusters in the triforium, possibly from the first church, with a pleasant use of diapered Roman tilework in the tympana on the south side (88). The great arches at the crossing are very fine, and give some solemn vistas; and here the decorative patterning of the arch-molds, that survives to some extent throughout the church, is most conspicuous and successful (88). At the third bay the quire is closed to the east by a tall, stately reredos of the fifteenth century, similar in type to those at Winchester and Southwark, once rich with figures, now inevitably replaced by modern work. Flanking it on either side are the beautiful fifteenth-century chantries of Abbots Wallingford and Ramryge.

In the small Saints' Chapel behind the reredos stands the pedestal of St. Albans shrine, its fourteenth-century canopy patiently pieced together from smashed fragments. It is flanked to the north

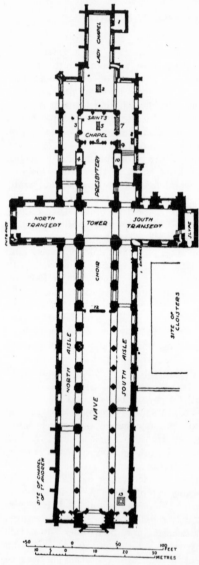

by a magnificent timber watching-loft of the fifteenth century, which is faced on the south by the large and splendid chantry of Humphrey, Duke of Gloucester, the youngest son of Henry IV. This Saints' Chapel, with the retro-quire to east of it, is roofed with a timber vault retaining much of its original colouring; but the latter has suffered appallingly from having had in the past a public passage driven through it. The Lady Chapel at the extreme east is a single-storey design of three bays, and for over two hun-dred years did duty as a Grammar School. It has consequently been almost entirely rebuilt, but with a treatment by no means un-sympathetic, and there is still sufficient to show, es-pecially in its lovely little statuettes and crocketed canopies, how delicately the style of the fourteenth century flowered at St. Albans.

At the Dissolution, the fabric remained with the Crown until 1553, when it passed to the city. Some traces of the cloister are visible against the south wall of the nave and south transept, but the monastic buildings have wholly disappeared with the exception of the great gateway to the west, dating from *circa* 1365 and long used as a prison.

87 ST ALBANS : A Springtime View of the Cathedral at the Crossing, showing the low Central Tower, largely built of Roman Tiles

88 ST ALBANS : The Great Arches of the Crossing, and the archaic
Triforium Arcade of the South Transept

89 ST ALBANS : The Interior of the Nave, the second longest in Europe, showing the fourteenth-century *Pulpitum*, and on the second pier from the left one of the early frescoes of the Crucifixion, formerly above a small altar

90　SALISBURY : A Distant South View of the Cathedral, rising above
the water-meadows of the Avon

SALISBURY

There is little that is obscure or even very eventful in the history of Salisbury Cathedral. The see was first founded in 1075 at the Roman fortress of Old Sarum a few miles away, but by the beginning of the thirteenth century the church had become so cramped and inconvenient that it was decided to build afresh on a new site, and work on the present cathedral was begun under the famous Bishop Poore in 1220. Nine years later Poore was translated to Durham, and following him in his train went the canon Elias of Derham, in whom some writers have recognised not only the architect of the beautiful Chapel of the Nine Altars at the latter, but also of the main fabric of Salisbury, though from an improved knowledge of medieval methods it seems hardly likely that his office was ever more than that of a modern clerk of the works. Work on the cathedral continued steadily under Bishops Bingham, William of York and Giles of Bridport, and in 1258 the building was consecrated with great ceremony in the presence of Henry III. The beautiful upper tower and spire were added during the first half of the fourteenth century, and with only the light arches at the crossing to bear their weight, were a perpetual source of anxiety until quite recent times, necessitating the building of flying buttresses and of the great internal girders at the crossing during the fifteenth century, and, in 1697, a competent strengthening of the whole structure by Sir Christopher Wren. In 1798 the great Wyatt was employed on a general scheme of 'restoration' that included not only the demolition of the sumptuous Perpendicular Beauchamp and Hungerford chantries flanking the Lady Chapel, and of the detached bell-tower that appears in old engravings, but also a ruthless opening up of 'vistas,' and the wholesale destruction of the remaining stained glass. In no other cathedral did the hand of this stucco-Gothic mandarin fall more heavily; but the work of falsification was by no means completed, and in 1862 came Scott, with an elaborate programme of works that left the interior in its present state of "encaustic floors, varnished marble and a quire bepainted and bedizened."

By some miraculous dispensation, however, the exterior largely escaped the restorers, and to-day the building appears much as it was left in the mid-fourteenth century, in surroundings that are perhaps the most beautiful of any English cathedral. The close is in itself an epitome of English house design at its best periods. Of the Tudor are the beautiful Church House and large rambling bishop's palace by the Avon, and among an adorable group of the Later Renaissance, little Mompesson House, with its delicate ironwork screen, is charmingly typical of the 'middling' house of the early eighteenth century. The cathedral, rising vast and shapely among trim lawns, is one of the few in England that can be realised

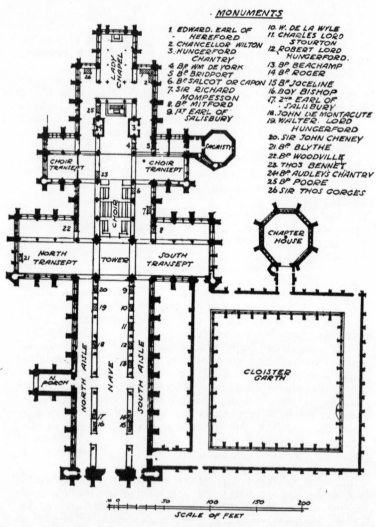

MONUMENTS

1. EDWARD. EARL OF HEREFORD
2. CHANCELLOR WILTON
3. HUNGERFORD CHANTRY
4. BP. WM. DE YORK
5. BP. BRIDPORT
6. BP. SALCOT OR CAPON
7. SIR RICHARD MOMPESSON
8. BP. MITFORD
9. 1ST EARL OF SALISBURY
10. W. DE LA WYLE
11. CHARLES LORD STOURTON
12. ROBERT LORD HUNGERFORD.
13. BP. BEACHAMP
14. BP. ROGER
15. BP. JOCELINE
16. BOY BISHOP
17. 2ND EARL OF SALISBURY
18. JOHN DE MONTACUTE
19. WALTER. LORD HUNGERFORD
20. SIR JOHN CHENEY
21. BP. BLYTHE
22. BP. WOODVILLE
23. THOS. BENNET
24. BP. AUDLEY'S CHANTRY
25. BP. POORE
26. SIR THOS GORGES

SCALE OF FEET

completely at the first glance and from many angles (91). But however varied the grouping, the general effect remains unchanged, of a lofty pile of warm-hued greyish stone, tinged with the green of lichen, rising by stages to the slender magnificence of the central tower; and exquisitely poised above all, the tallest and loveliest medieval spire in England, the fame and the glory of what Henry James called this "blonde beauty among churches."

This Salisbury spire, 404 feet high, is a landmark over miles of Wiltshire country. Constable loved to draw it as a calm central feature of his windswept compositions, and even the camera has not exhausted the range of viewpoints, and we see it afresh (90) rising slender above the water-meadows west of the city, where the tangled streams of Salisbury Plain combine in the Wiltshire Avon. United in exquisite harmony with the rich fourteenth-century craftsmanship of the central tower, its effect is indeed beyond criticism; the delight of the first impression is amply qualified at closer range. And if the main body of the fabric cannot aspire to this perfection, it does at least represent a complete and soberly expressive essay in the grand youthful style of the early thirteenth century—a realisation in warm Chilmark stone not only of the stylistic aims of the builders, but also of their new conception of the planning of an English cathedral. The solid strength and full, rounded curves of Romanesque give way to sharp angles and expanses of lancet fenestration (92, 100), and the ritual require-ments that insisted on an eastern Lady Chapel and double transepts resulted in a multiplicity of façades that should have provided ample scope for the decorative ingenuity of the designers. Yet despite its unity and cohesion, there is about the Salisbury design a lack of subtlety and suggestion of repetitive monotony that occasionally call to mind the machine-made frontages of post-war London: despite the lofty excellence of the proportions, a certain leanness in its range upon range of lancets and gabled buttresses, with, to relieve the excessive verticality, only a continuous arcaded parapet carried on corbels and the horizontal scoring of the buttresses at each stage. The west front was probably the last face to be com-pleted (91), and is one of the worst failures of its period. Designed purely as a screen, like the great fronts at Peterborough and Lincoln, it is lacking in much of the beauty and equilibrium of its prototypes, and remains a haphazard patchwork of buttress, arcade and win-dow, brought together with little sense of scale or texture. The three tall lancets that form the central feature, though necessary for lighting the nave, are entirely out of harmony with the variegated pettiness that surrounds them; and, to make matters worse, the statues that filled the hundred-odd niches have, with a few weath-er-worn exceptions, vanished, to be largely replaced by modern trivialities of the art workshops.

Swept and garnished by Wyatt and later by Scott, the long lofty nave of ten bays gains its chief effects from its cool emptiness, its astonishing perennial youthfulness (it might indeed have been built yesterday). Technically it is a triumph of finished masoncraft, rejoicing in its new-found use of Purbeck and deep-cut moldings; and the design is rendered throughout with a flawless precision that altogether rejects the more human craft of the foliage carver (93).

It is impossible not to admire the smooth dressing of the grey piers of Chilmark stone, with their slender applied stalks and crisply molded capitals of Purbeck, now darkened by varnishing. Above the steep arcade, the triforium is a broad and ample treatment of plate tracery and clustered Purbeck shafting; and between the tall triple lancets of the clerestory, the vault springs steeply to an even ridge line 85 feet above the floor, the loftiest of its kind in England. Though the western lancets in-clude some old fragments, the windows are almost entirely of clear glass, and the result is somehow reminiscent of a vast cistern, flooded to the brim with cool white light.

The light lofty arches of the crossing, on their slender clus-tered piers, would seem quite inadequate to carry the full weight of the tower and spire. But this they did for over a hundred years, till the cathedral showed signs of collapsing like a card-house, and the fifteenth-century masons, with their tal-ent for decorative shoring, con-trived, in *circa* 1450, the beauti-ful 'girders' of panelled mason-ry (96) to counter the inward thrust of the flying buttresses, as was also done at a later date across the eastern transepts with plain inverted arches. The view across the main transepts under these great girders is very beautiful, and here the glare is tempered by the insertion of excellent modern *grisaille* glass in the north and south windows. The lierne-vaulted canopy of the tower dates from the seventeenth century, but Wyatt's *pulpitum* at the crossing, made up of fragments from the demolished Beauchamp chapel, has been replaced by a characteristic metal affair by Scott and Skidmore. In the full polychromatic horror of its painting and encaustic tiles, to say nothing of a complete range of Scott fittings, the quire presents an unhappy spectacle, but a notable series of tombs has survived the restorers, including, on the south side, the fine thirteenth-cen-tury Bridport Monument, with its rich arcade of broken vigorous

GIRDER ARCHES ACROSS THE
EASTERN TRANSEPTS

91 SALISBURY : A South-West View of the Cathedral across the
smooth lawns of the Close

92 SALISBURY : A View from the Cloister Garth. The North Walk
screens the junction of the Nave and Transept

93   SALISBURY : Grey Chilmark Stone and Varnished Purbeck. A View
of the Nave from the South Aisle

94 SALISBURY : The Vaulted Roof of the Chapter-house, showing the Central
Pier and the Heads of the Geometrical Windows

95 SALISBURY : A Section of the Wall-Arcade of the Chapter-house, carved
with vivid little Scenes of the Old Testament

97 SALISBURY: The Retro-Quire and Lady Chapel, showing the attenuated stalks of Purbeck Marble that support the remarkable Multiple Vaulting

96 SALISBURY: The Great Arches of the Crossing, showing the Fifteenth-Century Stone Girder across the North Transept

sculpture, and, on the north, the two-storeyed fifteenth-century tomb of Bishop Audley (who also built his chantry at Hereford), with traces of original painting on its fan vault. Some interesting medieval ironwork from the demolished Hungerford Chapel was re-erected in the quire by Wyatt as a curious pew for the Earls of Radnor; and among a crowd of lesser tombs and tablets, mention must be made of the large and striking Renaissance monuments of Edward, Earl of Hertford, and Sir Thomas Gorges that now close the aisles to the east.

The retro-quire behind the high altar (97) forms a single composition with the small eastern Lady Chapel, the earliest part of the building to be completed; and here the multiplicity of single and compound Purbeck shafts which carry the steep intersecting compartments of the vault give an effect that is perhaps more curious than beautiful—in its flimsy attenuation not to be compared with the fine and somewhat similar work at Wells. The vast octagonal chapter-house, however, gives a real impression of airy spaciousness, due to the slender delicacy of the central vaulting shaft and the remarkable size of the fine Geometrical windows that almost fill each wall (94). Here also, in the thirteenth-century arcade that surrounds the interior, is a vigorous and prolific school of figure-sculpture, providing a range of some sixty delicious little scenes of the Creation and the Old Testament, as graphic and appealing as anything in English carving (95). The cloister dates from the same period (1263–1284), simple but quite effective in its disposition of an arcade of uniform Geometrical tracery beneath an expanse of plain wall—its four walks enclosing a pleasant green garth shaded by old cedars (92). The little octagonal sacristy of the same date adjoining the south-east transept has a fine oak roof supported by a central column. The close is entered through some beautiful medieval gateways.

IN THE SALISBURY CLOSE

SOUTHWARK

When Southwark was still a marsh, before the building of London Bridge, the priory of St. Mary Overy (variously interpreted as 'of the ferry' and 'over the river') was founded under the wing of Winchester as a House of Sisters, later transformed by St. Swithun into a College of Priests. The character of the establishment was again altered in 1106, when Augustinian canons were installed, who continued to serve the church until the Reformation. Though the fabric incorporates a few Norman fragments, the building emerged in

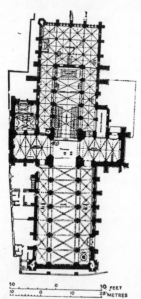

something akin to its present form during the thirteenth century under Bishop Peter de la Roche of Winchester, who, following a fire, remodelled the nave, and later the quire and retro-quire, in the current early-English style. After another fire in the fifteenth century, the south transept was rebuilt by Cardinal Beaufort at his own expense; and a few years later, in 1469, the vault of the nave collapsed, ruining the western limb. This was rebuilt with an oak roof, some of the heavy carved bosses of which are still preserved in the church; but after the Reformation, the building was allowed to slip gradually into disrepair, necessitating in the 'thirties of the last century a series of drastic restorations by Gwilt and others, in which the eastern Bishop's or Lady Chapel was sacrificed to the demands of a Bridge Committee, and the retro-quire only narrowly escaped the same fate. The nave was then reconstructed to the emaciated design that so enraged A. W. Pugin, but in the early 'nineties was demolished, and the present version built by Sir Arthur Blomfield. In 1897 the church was raised to collegiate status, and in 1905 it became a cathedral.

To-day it lies low and rather despondently by the river, hemmed in by railway lines and a jumble of Dickensian warehouses to the west. The exterior has been almost entirely renovated or reconstructed, but some notable features remain of the original design, including a striking thirteenth-century south doorway, some broad windows of uncusped Geometrical tracery, alternating with lancets, and the plain but quite dignified central tower, with its chequer-work parapet and rich corner turrets. On the interior, Blomfield's well-proportioned nave follows the lines of the quire design, and resembles the old nave as recorded by Dollman in general effect, if deviating in minor details. The transepts are picturesquely crowded with tablets and monuments; that on the north contains a magnificent inlaid chest presented in 1558, and opening from it on the east, the old vestry has been converted into a Harvard Chapel in memory of the University founder, who was baptised in the church in 1607. The unassuming thirteenth-century quire (99) contains no old fittings, but terminates in the rich stone reredos of Winchester type given by Bishop Fox, its canopies now filled with modern statues. East of it, the low rectangular retro-quire, divided by piers into twelve vaulting compartments, is perhaps the most charming part of the cathedral, a little reminiscent of that at the mother church at Winchester, but in its lightness and diversity of vistas more akin to Abbey Dore. There is a fine range of monuments, of which special mention must be made of the Jacobean group that includes the Gower, Humble and Trehearne tombs, each with its gaily painted effigy, recumbent or kneeling, attended by wives and ample progeny. Bishop Lancelot Andrewes, on the south side of the high altar, lies beneath a bright and flaunting canopy of early Renaissance type, and a word must be added for the magnificent brass chandelier of 1680 that lights the crossing.

FROM THE SOUTH-WEST

SOUTHWELL

Southwell Cathedral, like Ripon, originated as a collegiate church served by secular canons, and for centuries formed a supplementary bishopstool of the York diocese. According to Camden, who gives Bede as his authority, the first church on the site was built by Paulinus, the famous missionary bishop of York, during the seventh century. In the early years of the twelfth, the Saxon church was demolished and rebuilt under Archbishop Thomas of Bayeux; and the present fabric, with the exception of its eastern limb, dates almost entirely from this period. The reconstruction of the latter was begun early in the thirteenth century and completed about 1250, and the exquisite chapter-house (104), one of the flowers of English middle-Gothic, was added at the close of the same century.

To-day, the most striking exterior feature of the Minster is its west front, to which the conical spires, reconstructed during the last century, topping the severe and sparingly arcaded Norman towers, give a curiously Rhenish air. Between them is a vast Perpendicular window of many lights. The rugged design of nave and transepts, crowned by a low central tower (98), is relieved by touches of expressive detail, such as the string-course of bold zigzag ornament around the first storey, the cable and billet mold- ings of the aisle windows, the circular windows of the clerestory and the rich incised patterning of the transept gables. These tran- septs originally terminated in two-storeyed apsed chapels, which have disappeared; and adjoining that of the north is the detached octagonal chapter-house with its tall conical roof, beautiful without as within in its delicacy of tracery and detail (103, 104). The quire, with its miniature eastern transepts and foreshortened aisles, is a dignified design of tall lancets and lofty buttresses terminating in steep pitched gablets, with a touch of Lincoln warmth despite its general seriousness of demeanour.

The interior of the Norman nave has a certain stern effective- ness, with its heavy arcade of squat cylindrical piers, cavernous single-arch triforium and rather stunted clerestory that admits little light to the church (101). The aisles are roofed with simple quadripartite ribbed vaults in oblong compartments, and, as at Norwich, the triforium passage forms a virtual second storey of full aisle width. The nave itself was never roofed in stone, the present timber wagon vault having been added quite appropriately by Christian during the last century. The great arches at the crossing are lofty and effective, with their giant cable moldings, and the quire screen is one of the most beautiful of its type in England (101).

98 SOUTHWELL: The Long Low Profile of the Village-Cathedral of the Midlands, seen from the South-East

100 SALISBURY : The East End of the Cathedral, with the Gables of the Lady Chapel and Presbytery

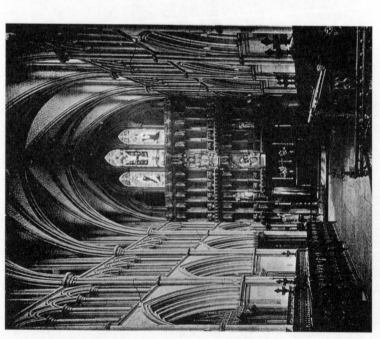

99 SOUTHWARK : The Quire, looking to the Stone Reredos, before its renovation with modern statues

101, 102 SOUTHWELL: The Heavy Romanesque Design of the Nave on the Left contrasts with the Slender Elegance of the Thirteenth-Century Quire. The fine Fourteenth-Century Screen is seen in the distance in the Nave View, and there is a glimpse of its richer eastern side in the picture on the right

104 SOUTHWELL: An Exterior View of the Chapter-house and its Vestibule

103 SOUTHWELL: The Rich Foliage Carving of Capitals and Arch-Molds on the Chapter-house Door

Built between 1315 and 1350, the eastern and western sides are
entirely different in design, the eastern, with its double tier of
cusped and crocketed niches, being of the two somewhat the
richer (102). The thirteenth-century quire has a dignity and simplicity that place it among the finest achievements of its period (102).
The carefully calculated design dispensed with a triforium, and the
tall glazed windows of the clerestory rise immediately above the
main arcade. The Lincoln influ-
ence is apparent in the rich corbels
of the vaulting shafts and in the
particularly low springing of the
vault itself; yet despite this pal-
pable lack of height, the whole
composition is so effective in its
proportions, so noble in its lighting, so aristocratic in its quiet
reserve of molding and detail, that
it produces an effect of spacious
serenity that definitely calls to
mind its great prototype.

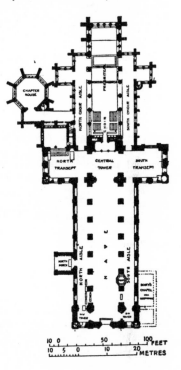

The chapter-house (104) is
entered from its vestibule by a
beautiful open tracery door. Octagonal in plan, its stellar-vaulted
roof is a triumph of Gothic
masoncraft, as at York dispensing
with the central pier, though here
the work is of stone throughout.
The continuous cusped arcading
of the walls is of a magnificent
elaboration in the carving of
capitals, crockets and arch spandrels
—one of the most remark-
able naturalistic displays to be
found in England. Nothing
is known of the master-carver responsible for this decoration, but it breathes a stronger personality than anything
else of its period, and there is a new imaginative freedom in the
rendering of foliage in endless variety and bird and animal forms,
with an almost uncanny skill in undercutting (103). This ornament
is applied in luxuriant clusters and festoons that are the antithesis of
the frozen stiff-leaf formality of thirteenth-century carving; and a
possible triviality in conception is outweighed by the astonishing
virtuosity in execution.

R

WELLS

Traditionally the first church of St. Andrew was founded at Wells as early as 705, but no historical records exist prior to 909, when the new see of Somerset was fixed at the little city beneath the Mendips. As a result of its promotion to cathedral rank, the church was soon afterwards rebuilt in stone, with a group of quasi-conventual buildings to house the secular priests who served it. This church probably survived into the reign of Stephen, when Bishop Robert of Lewes (1136–1166) set about its reconstruction with such vigour that a great Norman building was ready for consecration in 1148. But the splendour of the new church was short-lived. Little is known of Reginald de Bohun (1174–1191), save that he was an early friend of St. Hugh of Lincoln, whom he persuaded to come to Witham as prior of the first English Charter-house; but it is practically certain that it was under this bishop's direction that the remodelling of the building in its present form was largely carried out, on lines so revolutionary that the sureness and maturity of the design at its early period become a thing to wonder at. This Wells design does in fact represent a precocious and highly successful west-country experiment in Gothic before its time, that ranks with, and perhaps even surpasses in evolutionary significance, the work of St. Hugh at Lincoln or the Canterbury quire. It is hardly surprising that until quite recently it should have been attributed to the episcopacy of Jocelin some fifty years later, who actually was only responsible for the completion of the church on the same lines, with a laudable and scrupulous regard for the intentions of the earlier builders, and the addition of the magnificent west front. The cathedral may be said to have emerged practically in its present form under Dean John of Godelee (1306–1333), when the central tower was completed, the chapter-house raised on its earlier undercroft and the Lady Chapel added in 1326. The transformation of the east end was effected under Bishop Ralph of Shrewsbury (1329–1363), with the addition of the three eastern bays of the presbytery and of the beautiful retro-quire, forming a processional path between the Lady Chapel and the church. Here the work to all intents and purposes ceased until the nineteenth century, when the restorations of Salvin and Ferrey wrought considerable mischief, including the substitution by the latter of the present tasteless 'slate pencils' for the decayed Purbeck shafting of the west front.

Though the building to-day does not stand out in conspicuous magnificence like a Durham or a Lincoln, it is nevertheless one of the most beautiful in its setting of all the English cathedrals.

105 WELLS : A Distant North-West View of the Cathedral against the Green Wall of the Mendips

106 WELLS : A View from the High Ground to the South-East, showing the Grouping and Rich Texture of the Towers and Eastern Limb

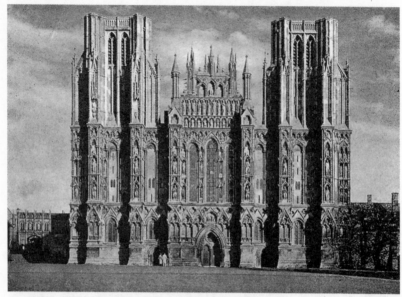

107 WELLS : The Sculptured Wall of the West Front, rising above the expanse of the Cathedral Green

108 WELLS : Detail of the Sculpture in the Central Gable of the West Front, showing the Twelve Apostles with a Tier of Angels above scenes of the Doom

It stands on the edge of a quiet village-town, almost literally in the shadow of the Mendips, whose steep wooded escarpment rises practically from the fringes of the close (105). Its west front is approached across green lawns (107); on the south side of it lies the Tudor bishop's palace, with its placid encircling moat and drawbridge gatehouse, and on the north, adjoining the chapter-house and Tudor deanery, is the grey backwater of the Vicars' Close, built for the Vicars Choral and forming one of the most complete domestic ranges of later medieval times. There is an extraordinary charm and repose in the grouping of these serene old buildings around the great church, whose fretted towers rise against a perfect natural background of green hills and woods (105, 106).

The most striking exterior feature of the cathedral is its west front (3, 107, 108). In the words of Professor Prior, "it is easy to see such a work as no framework of merely architectural designing, but as a whole piece of sculpture, and to recognise its object as not of aesthetic composition but of religious presentation." The Wells front does in fact represent a great screen of tabernacle-work, at the same time enveloping the free sides of the two towers, built to house the most remarkable display of medieval figure-sculpture in England, including a hierarchy of saints, priests and bishops, with kings, nobles, ladies and characters of legend and scripture (3, 108). The rich central gable is crowned by a mutilated figure of Our Lord in Glory, with, beneath, a splendid range of the Apostles, practically intact, above tiers of angels and a panelled representation of the Doom (108). In this purely sculptural conception, relief is provided by a range of six boldly projecting buttresses, which cast long angular shadows and bring depth and texture to the composition (3, 107). The elegantly buttressed towers were a fifteenth-century addition, and form a dignified architectural culmination to the rich variety of the earlier work.

The nave is plain in elevation, with Perpendicular tracery added in the lancet fenestration, and on the north side is a bold project-ing porch, curiously arcaded on the interior with interpenetrating moldings, finely carved in the spandrels. The transepts are of shallow projection, and adjoining that of the north is the substantial octa-gonal chapter-house, with its broad windows and rich parapet, and the delightful fifteenth-century bridge across the road that connects with the Vicars' Close. The central tower, though of no great height, is one of the most lovely and satisfying in England, dating from *circa* 1321, and, though simple in general treatment, finished with a delicate artistry of detail that compels real admiration. The east end, with the polygonal Lady Chapel and chapter-house, is the richest part of the fabric, designed with a broad elegance in its spacious fourteenth-century windows, flying buttresses and con-tinuous pierced parapets, that can be judged most effectively from the foothills of the Mendips that rise behind it, whence the view over the cathedral is of a serene and unforgettable beauty that can hardly be surpassed in England (106).

Within, the Wells nave is of eight bays, of which the four eastern represent Bishop Reginald's work. (5). With its closely spaced

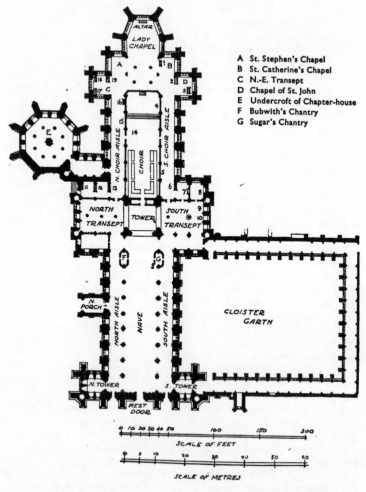

A St. Stephen's Chapel
B St. Catherine's Chapel
C N.-E. Transept
D Chapel of St. John
E Undercroft of Chapter-house
F Bubwith's Chantry
G Sugar's Chantry

piers, steep arches and deep-cut moldings, the design has a massive solidity, without heaviness, that is relieved by the delicate perfection of the carving of the stiff-leaf capitals, with its enchanting variety of interpellated figures and forms emerging almost insensibly from among the formal foliations. Of this fine school of early-Gothic sculpture it is only possible to mention a few famous examples, such as the cobbler, the fruit-stealers and their punishment, and the 'toothache' over Bishop Bytton's tomb in the south quire aisle,

which by association invested the relics of that worthy with a miraculous healing power over the complaint. The closely spaced lancets of the triforium form a continuous range from east to west that does much to accentuate the illusion of great length in the church, and the sharp springing of the plain sexpartite vault gives an impression of height inconsistent with the actual moderate dimensions.

But perhaps the most curious and distinctive features of the interior are the great inverted arches which have been thrown across quire, nave and transepts at the crossing (110). They were necessitated by the dangerous settlement of the main piers after the completion of the central tower, and their insertion (*circa* 1321) was a bold and structurally successful expedient which has been attributed to the innovating school of Severn masons responsible for the curious open

CARVED CORBEL ON THE CHAPTER-HOUSE STAIR

vaulting in their native cathedral (19), and later for the recasing of the Gloucester quire (8). The aesthetic success of these girders (which is all they are in effect) is a matter of opinion, but their

theatrical sensationalism is unquestionable, and a diagonal vista embracing three great arches, with their open spandrel eyes, at least provides a unique experience to the cathedral tourist. The fourteenth-century screen, reduced to. insignificance by Salvin during the last century, is largely obscured by this arrangement. East of it, the quire consists of the two distinct designs of Bishop Reginald and Bishop Ralph of Shrewsbury each of three bays to west and east respectively, unified by the delicate vertical remodel-

'TOOTHACHE' OVER BISHOP BYTTON'S TOMB IN THE SOUTH QUIRE AISLE

ling of the triforium during the fourteenth century, and the addition over all of a lofty vault, patterned with cusped lierne ribs, and in its proportions and detail one of the most beautiful in any English cathedral (111). The treatment of the triforium is as remarkable as it is successful. To all intents and purposes it forms a continuous range of rich attenuated tabernacle-work, from which unfortunately the statues have vanished; and in Bishop Ralph's three eastern bays the slender shafting descends deep into the spandrels of the arcade. In addition to the lofty Jesse window at the east end, four entire windows of the clerestory retain their old glass, but all the fittings of the quire are modern.

The polygonal Lady Chapel (*circa* 1326) is one of the most exquisite smaller works of English Gothic, and its range of tall windows still glows with something of the old richness of colour, though mostly a kaleidoscope of glass fragments (112). Its vaulting is a somewhat remarkable achievement, dispensing with the central pier and culminating in a boss carved with a beautiful figure of Christ in Glory. This Lady Chapel was planned as a separate octagonal block, and its later inclusion in the church was effected by a complex disposition of free-standing vaulting piers, with slender Purbeck shafts and richly foliated capitals, that constitutes the present retro-quire. Here, the varied vistas among the piers are of a singular beauty, each terminating in a deep glow of colour from the Lady Chapel windows (112). The aisle ends of the quire and the small eastern transepts form a group of minor chapels to house the bishops' tombs, of which the cathedral contains a notable series, including the rich Perpendicular chantries of Hugh Sugar and Bishop Bubwith in the nave.

From the north quire aisle, a passage leads to the thirteenth-century undercroft of the chapter-house, massively roofed with a low ribbed vault. The upper storey is approached from the north transept, where the astronomical clock, installed about 1390, is kept in working order, and "Jack Blandiver" still kicks his bell with great regularity at each quarter of the hour. A door gives access to the famous double-branching stone staircase leading to the bridge and chapter-house, and the latter is entered to the east through a graceful doorway of open tracery. Its interior is one of the most beautiful of its sort in any English cathedral (109), lighted by eight spacious traceried windows that fill the upper parts of each wall, and contain notable fragments of old glass in their heads. The central pier is built of clustered shafts of Purbeck, and from the capital springs a myriad-branching growth of slender ribs, caught in transverse lierne ties and studded with carved bosses. The cloister was built by Bishop Beckyngton, during the first half of the fifteenth century, between the south transept and south-west tower, and lacks a north walk. The same bishop was responsible for the three fine gateways in the close.

110 WELLS : The Great Girder-Arches at the Crossing, inserted to strengthen the supports of the Central Tower

109 WELLS : The Interior of the Chapter-house, looking to the Entrance Doorway

111   WELLS : A General View of the Quire, showing the Remodelled
Triforium and Lofty Elaboration of the Lierne Vault

112　WELLS : A Glimpse of the Lady Chapel from the Retro-Quire,
with its Kaleidoscopic Windows of Deep-Toned Medieval Glass

113   WINCHESTER : The Long Massive Profile of the Cathedral extended above the Roofs of the City.
A View from the South-East

WINCHESTER

THE CATHEDRAL CHURCH OF THE HOLY AND
INDIVISIBLE TRINITY

The history of Winchester reaches back to beyond the Roman Occupation, when Caergwent, in its cradle of chalk downs, was the most considerable settlement of Southern England. Here the Romans built a city, of which the importance lingered through the centuries that followed their withdrawal, until it emerged as the earliest capital of the Saxon kings. The ecclesiastical history of the place, as might be expected, is immensely long and complex. The original Saxon church, the shrine of St. Swithun, seems to have been much enlarged under Bishop Athelwold *circa* 963, who also added conventual buildings for the Benedictines. From this date until the Conquest the affairs of the abbey progressed tranquilly enough, and it was not until 1079 that the first important chapter in the history of the present cathedral began with the demolition of the old church by Bishop Walkelin, who laid the foundation stone of a vast new building on typical Anglo-Norman lines. This was formally consecrated in 1093, in the presence of almost all the bishops and abbots of England. It was very massively constructed, and its core, and parts of its actual fabric, continue to do service to the present day. Apart from the reconstruction of the central tower, which had collapsed, according to the fable, at the reception in the cathedral of the profane and impenitent carcase of Rufus, no further building work took place until 1189, with the accession of Bishop de Lucy, who extended the church eastward by the addition of a rectangular retro-quire in place of the Norman apses. But the greatest period of building, which saw the virtual transformation of the cathedral into its present mould, was schemed and tentatively embarked upon in 1346 by Bishop Edingdon, to be continued on a much more generous and stately scale under the famous William of Wykeham (1367–1404), whose courtly prestige and beneficence were equalled by his professional ability and enthusiasm as a builder. The founder of New College, Oxford, and of his own college at Winchester, the cathedral nave is a splendid memorial to his architectural discrimination. Willis describes his achievement succinctly in his Winchester monograph. "The old Norman cathedral," he writes, "was cast nearly throughout its length and breadth into a new form; the double tier of arches in its peristyle were turned into one, by the removal of the lower arch, and clothed with Caen casings in the Perpendicular style. The old wooden ceilings were replaced with stone vaultings, enriched with elegant carvings and cognisances. Scarcely less than a total rebuilding is involved in this hazardous and expensive operation, carried on during ten years with a systematic order worthy of remark and imitation."

The bishops who succeeded Wykeham continued his tradition, and Beaufort, Waynfleete, Courtenay, Langton, Fox and Gardiner, the first waverer of the post-Reformation line, who married Mary of England and Philip of Spain in the cathedral, all added their quota to its splendours, not least among which were their own tombs, that formed a splendid range east of the high altar, gracefully painted and chiselled. The fabric suffered little at the Reformation, but with the Civil War occurred a terrible violation of the interior by Parliamentary troops, that stripped its shrines, tore down its statues and smashed practically the whole of its old glass. Nineteenth-century restoration was slight and fairly insignificant, but at the beginning of the present century, signs of settling in the foundations necessitated a tremendous work of underpinning, which it is to be hoped has left the building sound and secure for many years to come.

Internally, Winchester Cathedral has come down to us as a splendid repository of medieval craftsmanship, enshrining a crowded ceremonial chapter in the national history. Externally it has to be admitted that its appearance is disappointing, and even its situation unremarkable in a city that contains as much of historic interest as any in England, including the fifteenth-century ranges of Wykeham's College, the large rambling Wolvesey Palace, with its beautiful brick hall of the Restoration, and the unique medieval group of Cardinal Beaufort's Hospital of St. Cross, finely situated above the green water-meadows of the Itchen. By contrast, the solid plainness of the cathedral comes as something of an anticlimax, lying vast and squat in a pretty close of lime avenues and sleepy reticent old houses (113). Edingdon's gabled west front of *circa* 1360 is a rather mechanical early essay in the new Severn style; and the longest nave in Europe is heavily built to a plain design, flanked by even ranges of ground buttresses, with reconstructed windows in aisles and clerestory of a delicate individual style of Perpendicular tracery known as 'Wykeham's type.' The transepts retain their Romanesque severity despite some later fenestration, and the low plain central tower does not form a very impressive culmination to the building's bulk. The eastern limb is the richest part of the fabric, with dignity and elegance in its crocketed Perpendicular pinnacles and flying buttresses. East of it, the thirteenth-century retro-quire forms a low extension, terminating in the graceful fifteenth-century reconstruction of the Lady Chapel.

On the interior, the contrast is immediate and impressive, and the view up the long lofty nave of twelve bays is as dazzling as anything in cathedral art (114). Here undoubtedly is one of the most eloquent works of English Gothic, a shapely and harmonious recasing that gives little indication of the massive core of Norman masonry that underlies it. Closely spaced and crisply molded into a multiplicity

114 WINCHESTER : A Fine Panorama of William of Wykeham's Nave, the
longest in Europe, looking East

116 WINCHESTER : The Heavy Romanesque
Fabric of the North Transept

115 WINCHESTER : Bishop Fox's Screen around the
Quire, with the Mortuary Chests containing the Bones of the
Early Kings and Bishops

of parts, the main piers barely suggest their actual immense
solidity (9); and an insistent sense of height is conveyed by the tall
vaulting shafts which form their inner members, rising slender into

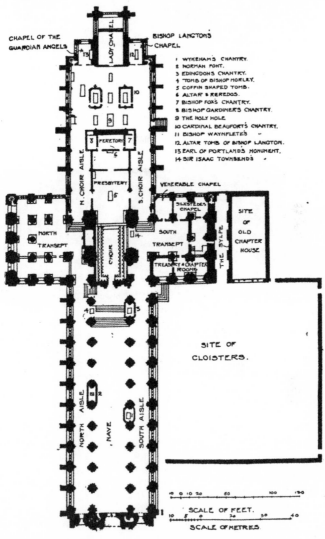

CHAPEL OF THE
GUARDIAN ANGELS

BISHOP LANGTONS
CHAPEL

1 WYKEHAM'S CHANTRY.
2 NORMAN FONT.
3 EDINGDONS CHANTRY.
4 TOMB OF BISHOP MORLEY.
5 COFFIN SHAPED TOMB.
6 ALTAR & REREDOS.
7 BISHOP FOX'S CHANTRY.
8 BISHOP GARDINER'S CHANTRY.
9 THE HOLY HOLE
10 CARDINAL BEAUFORT'S CHANTRY.
11 BISHOP WAYNFLETE'S   „
12 ALTAR TOMB OF BISHOP LANGTON.
13 EARL OF PORTLAND'S MONUMENT.
14 SIR ISAAC TOWNSEND'S   „

LADY CHAPEL

N. CHOIR AISLE

S. CHOIR AISLE

FERETORY

PRESBYTERY

VENERABLE CHAPEL

SILKSTEDES
CHAPEL

NORTH
TRANSEPT

CHOIR

SOUTH
TRANSEPT

THE SLYPE

TREASURY & CHAPTER
ROOMS

SITE
OF
OLD
CHAPTER
HOUSE

SITE OF
CLOISTERS.

NORTH
AISLE

NAVE

SOUTH AISLE

10 0 10 20   50   100   150
SCALE OF FEET.
10   5   0   20   30   40
SCALE OF METRES.

the clerestory, where small foliated capitals carry the springing
of the vault. Characteristically Tudor are the delicately panelled
spandrels of the main arches, and above them the triforium consists
of no more than a section of pierced parapet to each bay, carried

on a simple cornice enriched with heads and floral bosses. The lower lights of the tall clerestory windows are filled with stone panelling, and the vault is rich and complex in its patterning of lierne ribs and carved bosses. On the south side, the fifth bay is filled by the lofty Perpendicular screenwork of Wykeham's chantry (13), in which the fine effigy of the great builder is supported at the head by angels and at the feet by three curious little figures of canons, traditionally reported to represent his master-mason, master-carpenter and clerk of the works (118). Bishop Edingdon lies in simple dignity in the tenth bay; in the sixth on the north side is the square Romanesque font of black Tournai marble, carved with remarkable early reliefs of the life of St. Nicholas; and in the eleventh, just west of the crossing, an original Norman pier remains uncased as a commentary on the skill of Wykeham's masons (9).

ROMANESQUE RELIEF ON THE TOURNAI FONT. A SCENE FROM THE LIFE OF ST. NICHOLAS

In its stern archaic severity, the Norman work of Walkelin's transepts (116) forms a striking contrast to the polished brilliance of the nave. It is on a tremendous scale even for its period, and as a result of the collapse of the tower, portions were rebuilt in a conspicuously superior technique, with narrow mason joints and ashlar facing. A curious feature is the continuous aisle running around all three walls of each arm, forming a succession of small groined-vaulted chapels, with some interesting screenwork on the south side. Both transepts are ceiled with plain wooden roofs, and in the north, between the tremendous piers of the crossing, is the small recessed Chapel of the Holy Sepulchre, with its extensive traces of early mural painting. The ritual quire lies immediately beneath the crossing, which is roofed with a timber fan vault of 1634, and extends into the easternmost bay of the nave. The stalls are fine and intricate work of as early as *circa* 1300, incorporating much interesting figure and animal carving and a charming series of misericords; but it is characteristic of their period that their

117 WINCHESTER: A View in the Retro-Quire, showing the Chantries of Cardinal Beaufort *(left)*, Bishop Fox *(centre)*, and on the right Chantry's kneeling Effigy of Bishop Sumner

118 WINCHESTER: William of Wykeham's Effigy in his Nave Chantry. The monkish figures at his feet are said to represent his Master-Mason, Master-Carpenter and Clerk of the Works

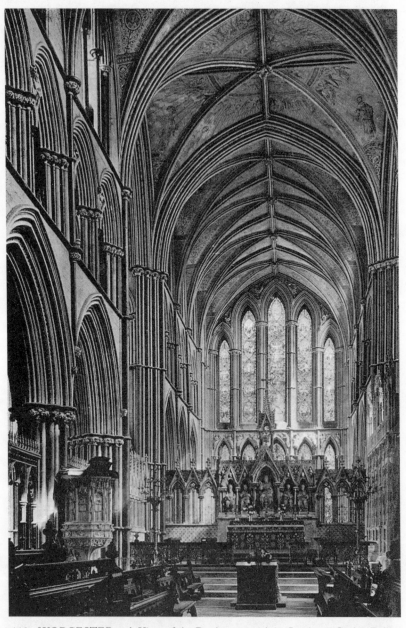

119   WORCESTER :   A View of the Presbytery, with its Jacobean-Gothic Pulpit
and Nineteenth-Century Refurbishments

general design is more akin to the craft of the stone-cutter than of the carpenter. Flights of steps on either hand lead up from the transepts to the presbytery aisles, that on the south closed by an iron grille of the eleventh or early twelfth century, originally made to shut off the pilgrims from St. Swithun's shrine, that is perhaps the earliest metalwork in use in England. This presbytery is of three bays, of which the piers and arches are simple work of *circa* 1320, with tall reconstructed clerestory windows of the fifteenth century above an elegant pierced parapet, forming virtually a two-storeyed design. The vault was built of timber in *circa* 1510, and its carved and painted bosses added in 1634. The beautiful stone screens that separate the aisles were added by Bishop Fox in the early years of the sixteenth century, and combine delicate Perpendicular tracery with Renaissance cornices that bear the six carved and painted chests containing the bones of the Saxon kings and bishops collected from the crypt (115). The stately stone reredos, contributed by Cardinal Beaufort, is almost identical in treatment with those at St. Albans and All Souls College, Oxford. Its intricate canopies have been preserved almost intact, but the figures are modern substitutes for those smashed by the Puritans in the seventeenth century.

Bishop de Lucy's retro-quire of *circa* 1200 forms an adequate if unassuming background for the magnificent series of tombs and chantries that are one of the cathedral's glories (117). Facing one another across the floor, and very similar in design, are the delicately aspiring canopies of Beaufort (1447) and Waynfleete (1486), the prince and the pietest. Fox's chantry on the south side is of a superb elaboration that surpasses either, infinite in its wealth of carved detail, and Bishop Gardiner's tomb of 1559 is practically Renaissance in treatment, though its tracery recalls the design of Fox's screen. Adjoining it, directly east of the high altar, can be seen the rich fourteenth-century canopies of the feretory that contained the cathedral's relics, with the exception of those of St. Swithun, whose shrine stood alone in the ambulatory. The eastern Lady Chapel is a Perpendicular reconstruction of Lucy's thirteenth-century work, which still appears in the first bay. Its fine spacious east window contains much old glass, but easily its most distinguished features are its simple sober wooden screen and stalls of the fifteenth century. Flanking it on either hand are two small chapels, on the north that of the Guardian Angels, with interesting roof paintings and Le Sueur's fine recumbent figure of Richard Weston, Treasurer to Charles I; and on the south Bishop Langton's chantry, filled with richly carved woodwork of *circa* 1500. The crypts are entered from the north transept and form an interesting commentary on the development of the Norman cathedral. The chapter-house and cloister have disappeared.

WORCESTER

THE CATHEDRAL CHURCH OF CHRIST AND THE
BLESSED MARY THE VIRGIN

While it is certain that Worcester was the seat of a Saxon bishop from the seventh century, little is known of its history until the tenth, when in 964 St. Oswald founded a new church there for Benedictine monks. In 1041 this church was gutted by the Danes, and in 1084 its rebuilding was begun on a larger scale by the Saxon bishop, Wulstan, who alone among English prelates retained his position for many years after the Conquest until his death in 1095. This second church had a chequered history. In 1113 it was seriously damaged by fire, and in 1139, in the reign of Stephen, occurred the curious raid on the city from Gloucester, during which the entire population, with its belongings, took refuge in the Minster. In 1175 the great tower collapsed, and in 1180 much damage was done by a second fire; but the present reconstruction may be said to date from *circa* 1140, with the building of the two western bays of the nave to a remarkably advanced Transitional design. By this time the fame of the canonised Wulstan had begun to spread through Europe, and his shrine at Worcester became a favourite place of pilgrimage. In 1207 it was visited in state by King John, but in 1216 the city embraced the cause of Louis against that despot, whose forces thereupon descended on it with considerable savagery, extorting so large a fine from the abbey that the feretory of the saint had to be melted down to raise funds. John, dying at Newark a few months later, left a caustic direction that his body should be buried in the church, between the shrines of its two saints, where it remains to this day. The rebuilding of the eastern limb was begun in 1224, and work on the cathedral continued by intermittent stages over a period of some hundred and fifty years, until in 1374 it may be said to have emerged in something akin to its present form with the completion of the central tower. Surprisingly small damage was done to it in the fierce siege of the 'Faithful City' during the Civil War, but in 1651, after the Battle of Worcester, the city was again occupied by the troops of Parliament, who confined 6,000 prisoners in the cathedral, plundering and damaging the interior. The building was virtually abandoned until 1660, when with the Restoration services were again resumed.

Despite excessive restoration that has almost amounted to a transformation of the exterior, Worcester Cathedral still stands quite impressively on the edge of a busy manufacturing town of rather slummy streets and restful dignified Georgian churches, and the tall gable of its west front and massive but delicate central tower form a fine composition from the green flats across the

Severn (120). There is a story that when Wulstan demolished the work of St. Oswald to build his new church, he was seized with remorse and exclaimed tearfully: "We wretches, pompously imagining that we do better work, destroy what the saints have wrought." No such scruples seem to have assailed the latter-day restorers of the cathedral, who cheerfully worked their will on its fabric for a continuous period of over a hundred years, beginning with Wilkinson, a local Gothicist, in 1756, and ending with Sir Gilbert Scott in 1874. The story is a not uncommon one in English ecclesiological history, of ignorant and ingenuous patching during the eighteenth century, followed by a destructive re-Gothicising

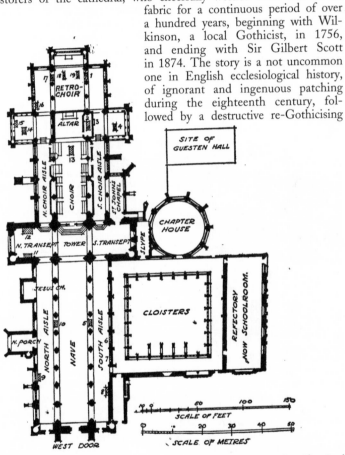

in the earlier part of the nineteenth, and a portentous 'purification' by some eminent church architect in the 'sixties or 'seventies. Worcester has suffered as much or more than any cathedral in this respect, and in the process has lost so much of its beauty and ancient character that there are few parts of it that call for very elaborate description in these pages.

Of the exterior, the central tower is the feature least spoilt by restoration (120), a dignified and well-proportioned work of *circa*

1370, with a rich Perpendicular upper storey. With its long nave and double transepts, the building covers a tremendous area, built of a pleasant brownish stone that to a certain extent mellows the traces of recent reconstruction; and of its varied façades, the west front is perhaps the most successful, with a vast Geometrical window between turrets that catches the long sunsets over the Severn (120). On the interior, the earliest and one of the most interesting parts of the church is the Norman crypt beneath the quire, which follows the lines of the original planning and is apse-ended, divided into a multiplicity of vaulting compartments by short crude piers with cushion capitals. In the main church, the earliest definite design is that of the two western Transitional bays of the nave, extraordinarily interesting work carried out, as has been seen, as early as *circa* 1140, with an attenu-ated triforium of graded trios of arches that seems to forestall plate tracery in the disposition of its rosettes of carved ornament. The importance of this work is empha-sised by later writers. "From Worcester west bays to Lincoln quire was a space of thirty-five years," wrote Professor Prior. "In the former, Gothic art is to be seen blocked out; in the latter finished and polished. . . . Its monoliths and the distinctions of coloured material foreshadow the uses of Purbeck; its triforium is a study for the double

THE TRANSITIONAL DESIGN
OF THE WESTERN BAYS OF
THE NAVE

arcadings, which played so large a part in the thirteenth-century style; and, finally, it has carvings and mold-sections, rough indeed, but still showing the path of Gothic sculpture."

The main design of the broad and spacious nave consists of seven bays of *circa* 1320, plain reticent work, though excellent in its proportions; and the main transepts represent a Norman fabric reconstituted in the fifteenth and much restored during the nine-teenth century. The quire (119) is a characteristic thirteenth-century design of clustered Purbeck shafts, well-carved capitals and multi-plied deep-cut moldings, with a triforium of coupled arches within a larger containing arcade, having a single sculptured figure in each spandrel. The clerestory, on its inner faces, consists of trios of graded lancets separated by slender shafts, and the vault, though

120 WORCESTER : The Cathedral from the North-West. A Summer View across the Severn

121　YORK: This View through the Nave and Quire conveys something of the remarkable
Scale of the Minster Interior

lofty, is of the plainest quadripartite type. The spacious dignity of
good proportions and lighting is marred, however, by the range
of tasteless and pretentious fittings, that must have caused a boom
in the 'art workshops' of the 'sixties and 'seventies. The simple
effigy of King John, on its beautiful fifteenth-century tomb, looks
decidedly overwhelmed, and the Jacobean Gothic of the pulpit puts
the rest to shame. The modern stalls incorporate some fine original
misericords.

The small eastern transepts, though each of only one bay, give
a curious effect of space and height, which is accentuated by the
lofty elongated lancets by which they are lighted. The lower walls
display a range of thirteenth-century arcading of plain type, which
is carried on continuously around the Lady Chapel formed by the
eastern bays of the presbytery, and provides in the spandrels a
series of really superb little carvings of scriptural subjects, including
vivid scenes of the Doom. In the south quire aisle, facing towards
the south-east transept, is the magnificent Perpendicular screen of
Prince Arthur's Chantry (12), commemorating the elder son of
Henry VII who died at Ludlow in 1502 and was buried at Worcester.
Its stone panelling incorporates a lavish display of Tudor badges
and emblems, including the rose, the portcullis and the Garter, and
the main vertical shafts, between areas of delicate open tracery,
are encrusted with enchanting little figures of saints and worthies,
standing half-revealed in richly canopied niches (11).

Worcester retains a fine Perpendicular cloister, roofed with a
continuous lierne vault that incorporates some good carved bosses
alternating with Angel sculpture. There is a well-preserved *lavatorium*,
only surpassed by that at Gloucester, and the chapter-house opens
directly off the east walk, forming on the interior a circular Norman
structure, richly arcaded, and revaulted in circa 1400 from a central
Norman pier. At this date the building, which had become dangerous, was reconstructed externally, and the large upper windows
inserted. Above the south walk rises the original refectory, dating
from the later fourteenth century and now used by the cathedral
school.

FROM THE SOUTH-WEST

YORK

THE CATHEDRAL CHURCH OF ST. PETER

The history of York goes back to beyond the Roman occupation, when the city first emerged as the principal settlement of the British tribe of the Brigantes. Under the Romans, as Eboracum, it grew to be one of the greatest military and economic centres of the island; and 'Altera Roma,' as it was called, was the temporary base of successive emperors on their visits to Britain. Despite the ravages of the Dark Ages, it was still a substantial Northumbrian settlement at the advent of Christianity, and in considering the subsequent building history of its cathedral, it must not be forgotten that, contrary to the usual conditions obtaining in England, the city did not owe its development to the building of a great new church, but rather had to contrive to accommodate one within its walls on a site that necessarily grew in extent as the cathedral was enlarged through the Middle Ages. This explains the comparatively restricted area of the close and precincts even at the present day.

With the consolidation of England under Edwin, York became for a spell the capital city, and it is at this period that its long ecclesiastical history begins. In 601 St. Augustine, with the papal authority, appointed twelve English bishops, including Paulinus of York, who was invested with powers to ordain further bishops as his evangelisation succeeded. While Augustine remained primate for his lifetime, it was laid down that for the future the dignity should be awarded between Canterbury and York by priority of consecration, thus sowing the seeds of the long and bitter controversy between the two sees that extended into the Middle Ages. Following the Norman Conquest, Aeldred, Saxon Archbishop of York, officiated at William's coronation at Westminster, earning for himself the contempt of most of his countrymen; but this timid prevaricator did not survive the uprising in Yorkshire of 1068, when the city was burnt, and the subsequent ravaging of the North by William, and a Norman archbishop, Thomas of Bayeux, was appointed to the see in 1070. The building of a new Norman cathedral was begun some ten years later, but of this it is probable that only the nave and transepts were at first completed. A new quire, and the present crypt, were built under Bishop Roger Pont l'Evêque between 1154 and 1181, but even when completed the church lacked the stature and splendour of the great Benedictine foundations; dissatisfaction with it came to a head some fifty years later; and its reconstruction on a scale commensurate with the dignity of an archiepiscopal see began with the rebuilding of the present transepts between 1227 and 1260.

It is difficult to grasp the tremendous scale of the Minster as it

122 YORK : The Minster from the South-West, showing the Rich Elaboration
of the Fourteenth-Century West Front and later Towers

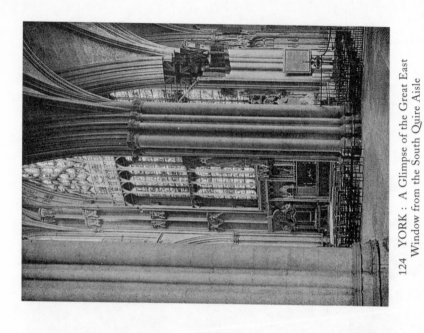

124 YORK : A Glimpse of the Great East
Window from the South Quire Aisle

123 YORK : The North Transept with the
Five Sisters Window

stands to-day from any one viewpoint in the town. The tangle of medieval streets that surround the close afford occasional glimpses of its three stately towers, but the best distance views are to be had from points along the old walls, where the dominant mass of the great church looms majestically above crowded rooftops. York is one of the largest of the English cathedrals, and one of the most consistent in that it expresses an almost continuous trend of later medieval development. With the exception of the crypt, it can show no work of a date prior to 1227, while the central tower was not completed until the early years of the fifteenth century. Between these dates, the slow current of building activity can seldom have been interrupted.

At close range, the cathedral presents some rich and varied façades, easily the most eloquent of which is the fourteenth-century west

THE MINSTER FROM THE SOUTH-EAST

front (122), of an elaboration hardly parallelled in English Gothic. It has been argued that its extravagant web of carved detail overloads the structural framework; at the same time, the proportions, in com-bination with the twin fifteenth-century towers, are sure and satisfying, and its exuberance is never monotonous. The Perpendi-cular eastern limb, with its skyline of crocketed pinnacles and curious open screens masking recessed clerestory windows, is on the whole distinctive and effective, though the inventiveness of the builders seems to have fallen short of the east end, where the design grows slightly mechanical. The gables of the thirteenth-century transepts form a striking contrast, terminating to the south in a magnificent rose window above ranges of characteristic arcading, and to the north, adjoining the chapter-house, in the tall lancets of the famous 'Five Sisters.' Above the crossing rises the largest central tower in England, a triumph of massive simplicity that ranks among the most spectacular constructional achievements of the fifteenth century.

T

Within, the crypt is all that survives of the fabric of the earlier Saxon and Norman churches, still preserving some distinctive Romanesque capitals. Above ground, the earliest existing work is

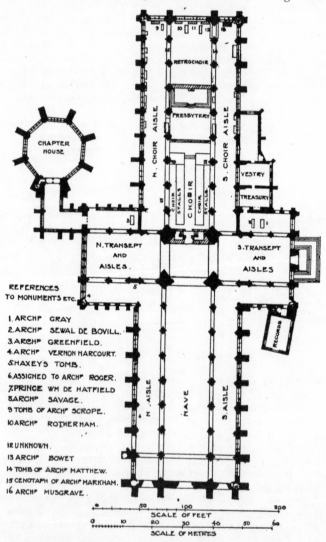

REFERENCES
TO MONUMENTS ETC.

1. ARCH⁺ GRAY
2. ARCH⁺ SEWAL DE BOVILL.
3. ARCH⁺ GREENFIELD.
4. ARCH⁺ VERNON HARCOURT.
5. HAXEY'S TOMB.
6. ASSIGNED TO ARCH⁺ ROGER.
7. PRINCE WM DE HATFIELD
8. ARCH⁺ SAVAGE.
9. TOMB OF ARCH⁺ SCROPE.
10. ARCH⁺ ROTHERHAM.

12. UNKNOWN.
13. ARCH⁺ BOWET
14. TOMB OF ARCH⁺ MATTHEW.
15. CENOTAPH OF ARCH⁺ MARKHAM.
16. ARCH⁺ MUSGRAVE.

SCALE OF FEET

SCALE OF METRES

in the transepts, which are built with eastern and western aisles. Conceived on as grand a scale as anything of their period (1227–1260), their proportions are open to criticism on the grounds of the heaviness of the triforium, which, though interesting and original in itself, is somewhat disconcerting to the scale of the main design. At the same time, the soaring height of the vault, with the deep flood of lantern-light at the crossing, gives an effect of lofty spaciousness rare in an English cathedral; and the views are magnificent, particularly that culminating northward in the solemn simplicity of the 'Five Sisters' Window, with its sea-green *grisaille* glass (123).

The highest and broadest cathedral nave in England, while impressive by its dimensions, is rather staid in general effect and lacking in ultimate distinction (121). Begun in 1291 and only finished in 1338, there is some rich and effective wall-arcading in the aisles, and the reserved Geometrical tracery of the windows is excellent of its type, if inclined to grow monotonous by repetition. The great curvilinear west window, however, is magnificent, only excelled by the rather similar creation in the east end at Carlisle. This nave, like the quire and transepts, was never completed with a stone vault; and in the case of the quire, the burning of the timber roof in 1829 was responsible for the destruction of the magnificent choir-stalls, which appear in Britton's engravings. Its interior design is a large-scale but not very distinctive version of Perpendicular, begun as early as 1361 and completed in the opening years of the fifteenth century. The last four bays were used as the Lady Chapel, and the east end is filled by an immense rectilinear window (124) which probably constitutes the greatest single area of fifteenth-century glass in Europe.

The octagonal chapter-house (1290–1310) adjoins the north transept, and by its great height, preponderant areas of glass, and perhaps also the absence of the characteristic central vaulting pier, as at Wells and Westminster, gives a superb effect of airy lightness. This absence, however, is a double loss, for the roof is the usual York version in wood. Nevertheless in its detail, its tracery, its beautiful *grisaille* glass, and, above all, its abundant naturalistic carving, the York chapter-house ranks high among the achievements of its period, and is not unworthy of the famous masons' inscription placed with affectionate pride beside the door:—

> Ut rosa flos florum,
> Sic est Domus ista Domorum.

But the chief glory of York Minster is in its windows, in which the steady development of English glass-painting can be traced through three centuries. No other great English church preserves so much of its original glazing, or conveys so fine an idea of the colour and glow of the interior in which medieval man delighted. Dating from the earlier thirteenth century is the beautiful *grisaille* of the 'Five Sisters,' with its delicate wreathings of foliage and narrow bands of pale colour; and the glass of the chapter-house, though slightly later in date, is also in *grisaille*, but here enriched with medallions and definitely warmer in its tones. There are almost continuous ranges of fourteenth-century 'band' windows in both the aisles and clerestories of the nave, among them the delightful 'Bell-founders' Window,' the gift of Richard Tunnoc, a bellfounder of the city, with its display of bells in borders and canopies, and the 'Heraldic Window' of Peter de Dene. The glass of the two great windows in the quire, incipient transepts, is devoted to the lives of

THE CHAPTER-HOUSE

St. William and St. Cuthbert, and the deep-toned fourteenth-century work of the west window faces across the length of the cathedral to the myriad-tinted sea of glass that fills the east end, completed in 1405 by John Thornton of Coventry, one of the finest achievements of this craft in England or all Europe, with its 117 exquisite biblical panels, ranging from the Creation to the Apocalypse, each about a yard square (124).

PARISH-CHURCH CATHEDRALS

The churches briefly described in this section were all of them raised to cathedral rank in comparatively recent years, most of them within living memory and several since the last war. In every case they were built principally for parochial use, and their promotion was consequent on the rapid industrial development of certain districts, and the vast general increase in the population during the last century. Though some are magnificent in themselves, they bear little relation to the cathedral art propounded in the introduction. Their inclusion is for the sake of completeness, and in certain cases it is quite impossible to do justice to their wealth of craftsmanship and mellow charm.

Birmingham.—This fine classical church, dedicated to St. Philip, was designed by Thomas Archer, a talented pupil of Vanbrugh, and was built between 1711 and 1719. The well-designed steeple is pleasantly characteristic of its period, and the wooded churchyard is a welcome patch of green amid the rather gloomy industrialisation of the city. The galleried interior (129), with its well-defined cornice and tall free-standing Corinthian columns to the east, is spacious and impressive, and the modern chancel is separated from the nave by a delicate ironwork screen, perhaps by the famous Tijou who worked for Wren at St. Paul's. Three great windows at the east, and one at the west, contain effective stained glass designed by Burne-Jones and executed by William Morris.

Blackburn.—St. Mary's is a spacious, well-lit and by no means contemptible production of the early Gothic Revival, built in 1818 from the plans of John Palmer. Its galleried interior has slight memories of both Southwell and Ripon. The dignified tower was a later addition.

Bradford.—This fine large 'wool church,' dedicated to St. Peter, dates chiefly from the fifteenth century, though earlier work is incorporated in the fabric, and the transepts are modern. The interior was 'classicised' with the fittings in 1704, and perhaps rather unfortunately restored to grace in 1899. There is a magnificent timber font-cover of the fifteenth century.

Chelmsford.—The church of St. Mary the Virgin is a large and dignified fabric of East Anglian type, for the most part built of flint (126). The vicissitudes of its history have left it with a nave rebuilt following a collapse in 1800, and a chancel much refurbished. The sturdy tower, with its small needle spire, and the Perpendicular south porch are easily the finest features, both enriched with flint 'flushwork' patterning.

U

Coventry.—The city's three great churches, Holy Trinity, St. John the Baptist's and St. Michael's, are all in the front rank of fifteenth-century achievement. The latter was chosen as the cathedral of the new see, but its appearance is typical of a splendid parish church in a rich and important medieval city, with an accumulation of chapels for the use of the many trade and religious gilds. In accordance with the aims of the period, St. Michael's is conceived as a great stone lantern, with preponderant areas of window (125); and a unique feature of the design is the pentagonal eastern apse, built to all intents and purposes of traceried glass and forming a radiant background for the altar. The tower is surmounted by a graceful octagonal lantern, from which a tall spire rises to 300 feet, only surpassed in height by those at Salisbury and Norwich.

Derby.—The tower of All Saints' is a tall fine example of late-Perpendicular building, dating from circa 1510, but the remainder of the church was demolished in a single night, following an acrimonious dispute with the Corporation, by order of the incumbent, the Reverend Dr. Hutchinson, a stalwart classicist, who enlisted James Gibbs to design a new nave and chancel, which were completed in 1725 under the supervision of Smith of Warwick. It is a graceful and pleasing interior (130) despite the efforts of late-Victorian decorators, and there is cause for real thankfulness that much of the magnificent Renaissance ironwork of the great local smith, Robert Bakewell, remains in the church.

Leicester.—The large and rather heterogeneous church of St. Martin contains work of many periods, but chiefly bears the stamp of the fifteenth century. Like most great town churches of its period, it can boast a remarkable accumulation of chapels, the largest and finest of which, St. George's, is placed rather curiously at the west end of the south aisle. The tower and broach spire were rebuilt during the eighteen-sixties consistently with Leicestershire type.

Manchester.—Though St. Mary's was collegiate as well as parochial, its appearance and arrangement belong exclusively to the latter category. It became a cathedral in 1848. The dignified tower is a modern reconstruction, but the main fabric, though the parapets and pinnacles were added of recent years, represents, like St. Michael's at Coventry, a splendid town church of the fifteenth century (128), with spacious ranges of Perpendicular windows, a fine open-timber roof and an accumulation of chapels laterally to north and south that forms, as at Chichester, a second pair of aisles. The interior effect is remarkably airy and graceful, but the chief glory of the church is its magnificent array of woodwork fittings, one of the finest achievements of late-medieval craftsmanship, comprising, in addition to the beautiful stalls, a rich wooden

125 COVENTRY : The Fifteenth-Century Church of St Michael,
now the Cathedral

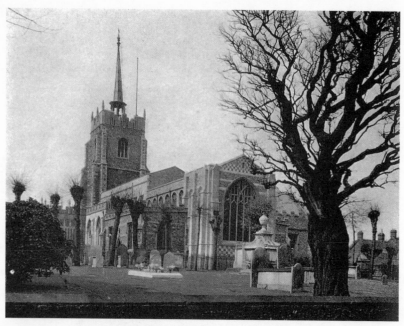

126 CHELMSFORD : The Church of St Mary the Virgin is of
several Periods, and largely built of Flint

127 ST EDMUNDSBURY : The Fifteenth-Century Church of St James, adjoining the Norman Bell-Tower of the vanished Abbey

pulpitum, now shorn of its rood and celure, and a splendid range of parclose screens in the chapels.

Newcastle.—Until promoted to be a cathedral in 1882, the parish church of St. Nicholas was among the four largest in England, a dignified fourteenth-century fabric, built of a dark stone, blackened by smoke, to which the stately tower of Scottish type, crowned with a rich pinnacle raised on flying buttresses, was added about 1470. Almost rectangular in plan from its accumulation of chapels, the interior, though dark, reveals some pleasant vistas, and there is a splendid timber font-cover of the fifteenth century.

Portsmouth.—The pleasant and interesting church of St. Thomas of Canterbury falls into two distinct building periods, the chancel and transepts being plain Transitional work of *circa* 1190, and the nave and western tower a reconstruction of 1683–1695. This latter, with its graceful crowning lantern and famous 'Golden Barque' weathercock, was built by royal command as a landmark and watch-tower against enemy ships. The delightful old fittings, largely made out of ship timber, have been inevitably somewhat 'cathedralised,' but there is a fine plain-panelled pulpit dated 1694, a fifteenth-century font and some beautiful Carolean plate.

St. Edmundsbury.—In the quiet Suffolk town of Bury St. Edmunds, the large Perpendicular church of St. James adjoins the Norman bell-tower of the vanished abbey (127). Despite drastic restoration, the long nave of nine bays remains a majestic parochial example of the mid-fifteenth century, but the chancel is a reconstruction of 1867. On the outside, the ranges of aisle windows and the three great windows of the west front are magnificent of their type, but the building loses in dignity from the absence of either a tower or steeple.

Sheffield.—The present quite dignified building represents a virtual reconstruction of the great Perpendicular parish church of St. Peter, effected in 1880 at a cost of £20,000. The Shrewsbury Chapel contains some fine Tudor monuments, but, with the exception of the fifteenth-century oak sedilia, the fittings are modern.

Wakefield.—The large plain parish church of All Saints shows a gradual evolution by successive remodellings from a simple early transeptal fabric with a central tower. This tower and the transepts have vanished and the church was largely reconstructed in the fourteenth century. The present western tower dates, however, from the early fifteenth, and the new eastern limb was added in the present century. The fine range of Jacobean fittings includes a screen, pulpit and font-cover.

MODERN CATHEDRALS

Truro Cathedral is probably the last considerable work of imitative Gothic to be built in England, having been consecrated in 1887 and only finally completed in 1903. Its architect, the late J. L. Pearson, R.A., designed it in distinctive version of the style of the thirteenth century, tinged with a French influence that is apparent in the general loftiness of its proportions inside and out (131), and in the attenuation of its towers and spires; and there is not a feature that has not its precedent somewhere in this country or in Northern France. To the modern eye, this unyielding literalism is the chief defect of the design, and the plan has all the intricacies of its thirteenth-century prototypes, and accordingly bears little relation to the requirements of English Protestantism. Ranking in its dimensions with Wells or Norwich, the spacious interior is treated with an admirable restraint and mastery of proportion, and the incorporation of part of the fabric of an old Perpendicular parish church to the south-east, adding a third aisle to the quire, results in some fine vistas. Generally speaking, there can be little doubt that Pearson's work is among the most impressive achievements of the later Gothic Revival, but despite its technical cleverness, its conception is inevitably anachronistic, and it never rises to the dignity of living architecture.

Liverpool Cathedral, on the other hand, is designed with an originality and free vision that are very refreshing, and on a plan far more consistent with modern cathedral requirements. Sir Giles Gilbert Scott's great work was begun in 1904; in 1910 the Lady Chapel was opened, and in 1924 the quire (132), and at the present rate of progress it should be well on its way to completion by the mid-nineteen-forties. The design has been considerably modified since its first preparation in 1901, in the architect's twenty-first year, but the accompanying drawing (133) gives an idea of how finely the cathedral will stand on its spur of high ground above a broken and picturesquely wooded quarry, with an old cemetery below. Overlooking the Mersey, to which its plan runs parallel, the building will form an imposing landmark over miles of amorphous dockland industrialisation.

Guildford Cathedral so far only exists in drawings (134), but Mr. Edward Maufe's design shows an effective simplification of Gothic forms, depending for its effect on the balanced grouping of plain masses, culminating in a bold dignified central tower. It will be finely situated on high downland overlooking the pleasant old town, whose red-brick Georgian church of the Holy Trinity is the present temporary seat of the bishopric.

128 MANCHESTER : The fine Fifteenth-Century Church of St Mary, in the middle of the great manufacturing city

129 BIRMINGHAM : The Interior of St Philip's, by Archer. The windows of the modern chancel are by Burne-Jones

130 DERBY : James Gibbs' Interior of All Saints', with the Ironwork Screens of Robert Bakewell

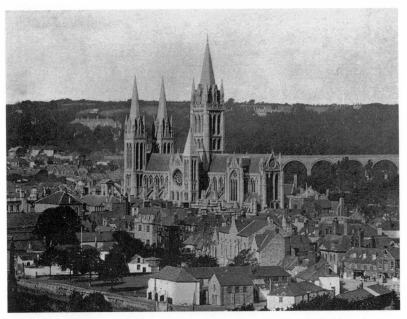

131 TRURO : The Cathedral, completed in 1903 to the Design of
J. L. Pearson, R.A.

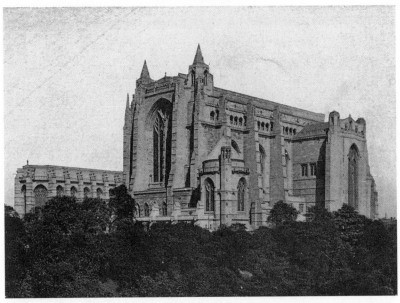

132 LIVERPOOL : The Completed Quire and Lady Chapel of the New
Cathedral. Sir Giles Gilbert Scott, R.A., *Architect*

133   LIVERPOOL : A Drawing by Raffles Davison of the Design of Sir Giles
Gilbert Scott as it will appear completed

134   GUILDFORD : A Sketch of Edward Maufe's Design for the New Cathedral

GLOSSARY OF TERMS USED

Defined as they apply to the Architecture of the Middle Ages

AMBULATORY.—The processional passage around a presbytery formed by the extension of the quire aisles.

APSE.—A semicircular or polygonal east end to a church.

ARCADE.—A range of arches supported by columns or piers, either open or 'blind,' i.e. closed with masonry. Arcading was often used as wall-strengthening decoration. (See *Wall-Arcade*.)

BARREL VAULT.—A covering of either stone or brick, generally of semicircular section. (Also known as *Wagon Vault*.)

BOSS.—In ribbed vaulting, a stone, usually carved with foliage or figures, occurring at the intersection of ribs.

BUTTRESS.—Masonry built out to strengthen a wall and to resist thrust.

CAPITAL.—The crowning member of a column or pier, giving support to superimposed arches or vaulting ribs.

CHANTRY CHAPEL.—A chapel within or attached to a church, endowed for the saying of Masses for the soul of the testator or others.

CHAPTER-HOUSE.—The council-chamber of a monastic or cathedral establishment.

CHEVET.—The apsidal group at the east end of a church, containing an ambulatory giving access to a sequence of radiating chapels.

CLERESTORY.—The side wall of a church above the aisle roof and nave arcade, always pierced with windows.

CORBEL.—A block, usually molded or carved, projecting from a wall and supporting a superincumbent weight.

CORBEL-TABLE.—A connected range of corbels immediately beneath the roof of a building; it can also support a parapet.

CRESTING.—Continuous ornament, carved or pierced, surmounting a screen, canopy or cornice.

CROCKETS.—Decorative features occur-ring principally at the angles of canopies, pinnacles and spires; usually carved and placed equidistantly.

CURVILINEAR STYLE OR TRACERY.—The first phase in the style of the fourteenth century, in which Geometrical

forms in tracery were superseded by flowing lines. (Also called *Flowing Tracery*.)

CUSPS.—In tracery, the small inner members that constitute the foliations in the form of trefoils, quatrefoils, etc.

DOG-TOOTH ORNAMENT.—An ornament in the shape of small four-leaf pyramids often set in a hollow molding, and repeated either continuously or at short intervals in thirteenth-century work.

FAN VAULT.—The final development in England of Gothic vaulting, in which the curve of all the ribs is similar. The actual ribs are generally decorative rather than structural, and the fan-like shapes, or *conoids*, are always apparent. Sometimes pendants are introduced.

FERETORY.— The part containing the relics in a shrine or monument.

FLYING BUTTRESS.—A buttress in the form of an open arch directing the thrust of a high vault across the roof of an aisle to the main buttress.

GEOMETRICAL STYLE OR TRACERY.—The phase after Early English, or Lancet, at the close of the thirteenth century, characterised by an early type of bar tracery designed strictly in geometric forms, in which circles and triangles predominate.

GROINED VAULT.—A vault resulting from the intersection of two or more surfaces at an angle, the 'arrises,' or lines of intersection, being the groins.

HAMMER-BEAM ROOF.—A wooden roof in which the tie-beam is dispensed with, and its place taken by projecting beams. The ends of these are generally treated decoratively.

LANCER WINDOW.—A name applied to the narrow pointed window of Early English Gothic from its resemblance to a lancet blade.

LIERNE RIBS.—Small connecting ribs used in vaulting, particularly during the fourteenth century, for decorative effect only.

MISERICORD.—The lifting seat of a quire stall, usually with a carved bracket on the underside. (Also known as *Miserere*.)

MOLDINGS.—The varieties of contour

given to angles, arches and other projecting members of various parts of buildings to produce contrasts of light and shade and richness of effect.

MULLIONS.—The vertical divisions between lights in a Gothic window, from which the tracery springs.

NAVE.—The western limb of a church, used by the secular congregation.

NORMAN ARCHITECTURE.—The English variant of Romanesque in the eleventh and twelfth centuries, immediately preceding Gothic.

OGEE.—A curve of double flexure, produced by a convex and concave curve flowing the one into the other.

PARCLOSE.—A screen separating a chapel or aisle from the body of the church.

PERPENDICULAR.—The last of the great periods of English Gothic architecture. It flourished during the later fourteenth, fifteenth and sixteenth centuries.

PIER.—A supporting member from which arches or vaulting spring, in form usually cylindrical, octagonal, rectangular or clustered, i.e. composed of a collection of shafts.

PINNACLE.—A tapering terminating member, vertical, and usually crowned by a finial, and smaller than a turret.

PISCINA.—A recess including a shallow stone basin, with a drain, set in a niche south of an altar for washing sacred vessels.

POUPÉE-HEAD.—The carved termination of a quire-stall or other bench-end. (Sometimes called a *Poppy-head*.)

PRESBYTERY.—The eastern portion of a church beyond the quire, containing the high altar.

PULPITUM.—The gallery above the solid screen separating the nave from the ritual quire in a cathedral or monastic church. The term is often applied to the screen itself.

QUADRIPARTITE.—A simple form of ribbed vaulting, consisting of transverse, diagonal and wall ribs, dividing a rectangular vault space, or compartment, into four segments or 'severys.'

QUIRE.— The part of the church between the screen and the presbytery containing the stalls of the monks or canons. The spelling 'choir' is often used, and the term is sometimes applied loosely to the entire eastern limb of the church.

RETRO-QUIRE.—The portion of the eastern limb behind the high altar to the east.

RIB.—A structural member dividing up the compartment of a vault, generally molded.

ROMANESQUE.—The style of architecture prevalent in Western Europe from about the ninth to the twelfth century, perpetuating the round arch of the Romans.

SEDILIA.—Recessed seats for priests on the south side of the high altar, generally of masonry and canopied.

SEXPARTITE.— A form of ribbed vaulting, similar to the quadripartite, but having an extra transverse rib which divides the rectangular compartment into six segments.

SHAFT.—A smaller column, either independent or a member of a pier.

SPANDREL.—The triangular space formed between two arches, or between one arch and the rectangular lines of a hood-mold.

STRING COURSE.—A projecting horizontal band or molding on a wall, often continued around a building.

TABERNACLE-WORK.—The carved and ornamental canopy-work over quire-stalls, fonts, niches, etc.

TRACERY.—The ornamental stonework in the heads of Gothic windows, springing from and supported by the mullions. Circular windows were also filled with tracery. The earliest form is *Plate Tracery*, consisting of circles and other geometrical figures cut in solid stonework. After the middle of the thirteenth century, the tracery was built up of stone bars (*Bar Tracery*).

TRANSOMS.—The horizontal bars in windows.

TRANSEPTS.—The cross-arms of a church, projecting transversely to the nave, presbytery and aisles.

TRIFORIUM.—The storey above the arcade, enclosed by the roof of a side aisle. In cathedrals, it is often a gallery between the arcade and the clerestory.

TYMPANUM.—The space enclosed between the lintel and the arch of a doorway in Norman and Gothic buildings, often filled with sculpture.

VAULT.—Any form of arched roofing over a building with the exception of the domical. Vaults are either groined, as in Romanesque architecture, or ribbed, as in all Gothic architecture.

WALL-ARCADE.—A blank, or 'blind,' arcade, used as a form of wall strengthening or decoration, and often richly carved.

INDEX